Key Topics in Identity Development

Who am I, and where am I going in life? This book explores the fascinating study of identity development, addressing how people navigate these fundamental questions throughout their lives. In an increasingly complex and globalized world, where choices and information abound, the book provides a comprehensive introduction to the foundations, theories, and applications of identity development, offering readers valuable insights into how we form our understanding of who we are.

Readers will gain essential knowledge on identity development, including its foundations, key theories, and methods of measurement, with opportunities to try widely used questionnaires themselves. The book also examines how identity research informs policy and addresses current and emerging topics in the field. By connecting identity development to interpersonal relationships, mental health, career choices, and professional growth, readers will discover how this knowledge can be applied to enhance their understanding of themselves and others.

This book is ideal for students in psychology, youth studies, pedagogical science, child study and human development, and family studies programs. It provides an accessible and engaging introduction to identity development, making it a valuable resource for anyone seeking to understand the lifelong process of navigating life paths and making meaningful choices.

Theo A. Klimstra is a Teaching Professor in the Eliot-Pearson Department of Child Study & Human Development at Tufts University. His research explores personality and identity development in adolescence and young adulthood, focusing on their connections to adjustment and well-being. He is interested in understanding why individuals develop differently, how they shape their life paths, and what factors contribute to flourishing or struggling.

BPS Key Topics in Psychology

British Psychological Society

Routledge, in partnership with the British Psychological Society (BPS), is pleased to present *BPS Key Topics in Psychology*, a series of short introductory books that focus on a specific field within psychology. Each book is broken down into bitesize chunks to provide a helpful overview of core psychology topics, made clear by a five-part structure: foundations, theories, methodologies, impacts, and emerging areas. Written by active and experienced authors, these essential books encourage students to approach fundamental concepts with confidence and critical thinking.

Books may incorporate student-friendly pedagogies, including tools such as: feature boxes; key terms and definitions; and links to further reading online. Concise yet comprehensive, these books offer a simple and accessible overview of core psychology topics for students looking for a summary of key concepts in the topic, or those new to the area.

Key Topics in Counselling Psychology
Terry Hanley and Laura Anne Winter

Key Topics in Clinical Neuropsychology
Sara da Silva Ramos, Dr. Christopher Byrne and Rudi Coetzer

Key Topics in Memory
Richard J. Allen and Charity Brown

Key Topics in Parenting and Family Psychology
Alina Morawska & Amy E. Mitchell

Key Topics in Identity Development
Theo A. Klimstra

For more information about this series, please visit: www.routledge.com/BPS-Key-Topics-in-Psychology/book-series/BPSKTP

"In this important book, Theo Klimstra provides a comprehensive and integrative review of theories and empirical research into identity development. It describes the various patterns of identity formation in an understandable way. The book is a significant achievement, and its findings will move the field forward."

Wim Meeus, *Emeritus Professor of Developmental Psychology, Utrecht University, The Netherlands*

"This volume introduces the reader to the landscape of psychological research on identity development. Written in an accessible, even humorous, style, Klimstra covers theoretical and methodological approaches to identity development, as well as established and emerging research. At the same time, he deftly offers critiques and challenges to how we think about identity development, which are sure to inspire good conversation and reflection for readers. This volume will serve as a clear and rich introduction to anyone interested in the study of identity development."

Kate McLean, *Professor of Psychology, Western Washington University, Bellingham, USA*

"Key Topics in Identity Development is an engaging textbook specifically written for undergraduates, regardless of their majors or areas of specialisation, who are interested in learning about identity development in general and in reflecting on their own identity. Klimstra has written in an inviting style, addressing the reader directly, locating himself in the context of his own heritage, as well as current circumstances, and with a touch of humour! Key topics are presented succinctly, enabling breadth of coverage, ranging from historical foundations of the study of identity to current and emerging areas of interest, such as identity development in the digital age."

Jayanthi Mistry, *Professor in the Department of Child Study and Human Development, Tufts University, Medford, USA*

Key Topics in Identity Development

Theo A. Klimstra

Routledge
Taylor & Francis Group
LONDON AND NEW YORK

Designed cover image: Getty Images

First published 2027
by Routledge
4 Park Square, Milton Park, Abingdon, Oxon OX14 4RN

and by Routledge
605 Third Avenue, New York, NY 10158

Routledge is an imprint of the Taylor & Francis Group, an informa business

British Library Cataloguing-in-Publication Data
A catalogue record for this book is available from the British Library

Library of Congress Cataloging-in-Publication Data
Names: Klimstra, Theo A. author
Title: Key topics in identity development / Theo A. Klimstra.
Description: Abingdon, Oxon ; New York, NY : Routledge, 2027. | Series: BPS key topics in psychology | Includes bibliographical references and index.
Identifiers: LCCN 2026007604 (print) | LCCN 2026007605 (ebook) | ISBN 9781032903606 hardback | ISBN 9781032902159 paperback | ISBN 9781003557593 ebook
Subjects: LCSH: Identity (Psychology) | Developmental psychology
Classification: LCC BF697 .K585 2027 (print) | LCC BF697 (ebook)
LC record available at https://lccn.loc.gov/2026007604
LC ebook record available at https://lccn.loc.gov/2026007605

ISBN: 978-1-032-90360-6 (hbk)
ISBN: 978-1-032-90215-9 (pbk)
ISBN: 978-1-003-55759-3 (ebk)

DOI: 10.4324/9781003557593

Typeset in Galliard
by Apex CoVantage, LLC

Access the Support Material: www.routledge.com/9781032902159

Contents

Section 1

Key foundations

By the end of this section, you will:

- Have an understanding of what identity is and isn't.
- Know about how culture is defined and how culture plays into identity and its development.
- Be able to name important moments in the history of the study of identity development.

DOI: 10.4324/9781003557593-1

Chapter 1

The foundations of identity development

The neighborhood I live in is near Boston and hosts a whole lot of people from a variety of backgrounds. Among my least favorite people are the ones yelling into their phones as they walk past, but most people are much more pleasant! For example, there are the two crossing guards who brave muggy, sticky, summer heat and brutally cold and windy winter days to help children get to school safely, check in on children when they haven't seen them for a couple of days, and still find the time to make sure that I don't get run over either. When the pedestrian light is red and there aren't any children waiting, we talk about the weather, the perks and annoyances of our jobs, or really anything that comes to mind. Another one is our cheerful neighbor who sees me with my laptop on the porch on sunny work-from-home days and asks me when I will finally get an actual job. He has been living in the neighborhood for much of his life and saw it going from an affordable working-class area to a place where buying a house has become something for the happy few.

Those are just some of the current residents. In the late 1980s and early 1990s, a Harvard Law School student who would become the 44th president of the United States, Barack Obama, lived right on the corner of our street. But around that time the neighborhood was also the home of a gang led by one of the most notorious gangsters of the 20th century: Whitey Bulger. The 2015 movie *Black Mass* directly portrays him, and the 2006 movie *The Departed* is also loosely based on him and his gang. But did Whitey Bulger see himself as a gangster? Barack Obama's autobiography surely doesn't suggest he saw himself as a future president when he lived here. And how about the crossing guards and our neighbor? Just because I describe them the way I do, doesn't mean that that's how they see themselves!

Questions about how people see themselves, their values, how they reflect on their "big" roles in life, and the choices for those roles are all relevant to understanding their identity development. This chapter first discusses what identity is and isn't about. The second part addresses the

DOI: 10.4324/9781003557593-2

question of what is and isn't considered development. The chapter ends with a conclusion on what identity development is about.

What is identity?

It's not easy to give a very exact definition of identity. Unfortunately, there is quite some unclarity on what people refer to with "identity", and this unclarity ranges from descriptions in popular media to those that are used in the scientific literature. That doesn't sound like a great way to start but fortunately attempts have been made to create some order in this apparent chaos.

Defining identity

At a basic level, **identity** is about people's responses to the question "who am I?" (Vignoles et al., 2011). It could also involve responses to questions like "who are we?" or "that's not who we are, right?", which you may have heard in discussion about the purpose and values of a particular group of people. Answers to "who are we?" questions are therefore relevant to something we call a group identity.

> **Identity** Informally, it is about people's response to the question "who am I?" or "who are we?". Formally, it is the part of your self-definition that provides you with a sense of sameness and continuity across time and place.

Those were the simple versions of the definitions. To get more precise, we will dive into the writings of someone who is widely regarded as one of the founders of the study of identity: Erik Erikson. He described identity as that part of your self-definition that provides you with a sense of sameness and continuity across time and place (Erikson, 1950/1993). **Continuity** refers to the notion that the person you think you are today, is pretty much the same person that you thought you were yesterday, and that tomorrow you'll still feel like you'd be largely that same person. At the very least, continuity refers to feeling like your past, present, and future selves are logically related to each other. A second function of an identity

> **Continuity** (as in "sense of continuity") The feeling that your present, past, and future selves are logically related to each other.

is that it provides a sense of **coherence** across roles and contexts. That doesn't mean you have to be the exact same version of yourself in every situation! It does imply that things like a stage persona (for example my teaching persona, who's a lot louder than my writing persona) or an in-game or online character serve as temporary roles, versions of yourself that are part of a broad repertoire. Coherence thus implies that you don't see taking on those personas as temporary transformations into someone who is completely distinct from "you".

> **Coherence (as in "sense of coherence")** The feeling that different versions of you (for example your video game character or [other] online character and the version of you who reads this book) are all part of a broader repertoire of who you are, and that these different versions of you are all logically linked to each other.

Continuity and coherence clearly feature Erikson's definition of identity, but there is a third function of identity: it provides us with a sense of **distinctiveness** (Pasupathi, 2014). In other words, it allows us to define ourselves as unique relative to others. It is based on our ideas about what we look like, how we'd describe our personality or character, our social status, our abilities, and basically anything else that we can use to distinguish ourselves from others. Distinctiveness might sound like a very individualistic concept, but it can also take the shape of someone describing their own unique contribution to their community. The idea is that to feel coherence and continuity, you first need to feel distinctive. In other words, you need something that is really "you" as a basis, and then you can have a sense of continuity and coherence related to that.

> **Distinctiveness** The extent to which you see yourself as unique relative to others. This does not imply that you see yourself as better or worse than others! It's just about seeing yourself as at least somewhat different and therefore distinct.

The "what" of identity

The definition and description of key functions of identity narrows things down a little bit for what would and would not be considered identity. However, there are a whole lot of words that you can put in front of

Identity domains A particular part of people's identity, such as their ethnic identity, gender identity, career identity, school identity, etc.

the word "identity", so there's many different identities. The broader scientific literature covers a wide range of such **identity domains**, or parts that may be relevant to how people describe themselves.

Perhaps some of the most widely discussed identity domains are those related to social categories such as gender, sexual, ethnic, and racial identity. Feelings towards where you are geographically may also translate into identity features, like regional identity, national identity, and identities referring to larger supranational regions (e.g., European identity). Other parts refer to social roles, such as student identity, teacher identity, athlete identity, identities related to hobbies/interests, particular roles played online, and occupational identity, or (roles in) social relationships such as various forms of interpersonal identity and parental identity. On top of that, there are also ideological positions that can be examined from an identity perspective, as there is research on political identity, religious identity, and moral identity. Instead of focusing on one, several, or all of these different parts of identity, there is also a common focus on people's general sense of identity, which refers to whether or not you feel like your general idea of who you are gives you a sense of distinctiveness relative to others, coherence across contexts and situations, and continuity across time.

It would be impossible to cover every single identity domain in this book. That would require something like the almost 1,000 pages in the two-volume *Handbook of Identity Theory and Research* (Schwartz et al., 2011). I strongly recommend checking out handbooks if you want to know more about specific topics, but this book you're reading right now provides an introduction to the more general approaches to identity with a focus on areas and topics that are typically covered in developmental science or developmental psychology. Specific identity domains or combinations thereof will only be used to explain these more general approaches.

References to specific domains are also helpful for further clarifying what is typically considered when investigating identity. Take, for example, ethnic identity. It is not uncommon to only refer to self-identification labels, such as African American, Welsh, Pakistani British, Romani, or in my case Frisian Dutch, when describing ethnic identity. However, Umaña-Taylor (2011) summarized an opinion held by many who study ethnic identity: to study it appropriately it should not be reduced to only a label as that would lead to overlooking important variability within groups. It's crucial to also ask questions about things like the degree to which people have explored what their ethnicity means to them and how much they feel part of the group they identify with. This doesn't only apply to ethnic identity as similar concerns arise when other identities are reduced to just a label. According to Erikson's (1950/1993) take on identity, identifying with a label without any exploration of how you feel about it or comparisons to alternatives, would not even be considered having an identity, but an **identification**. So, without any information beyond labels, we don't know whether we're dealing with an identity or identification. To learn more about people's identities and the development thereof, several specific aspects of identity are distinguished. Those represent what could be referred to as the "how" of identity.

> **Identification** In Erikson's (1950/1993, 1968/1994) work on identity, something you identify with without having reflected on it and/or without having explored alternatives.

The "how" of identity

To understand what the study of identity development is about it is important to briefly outline what concepts of identity are studied. All those concepts are pretty complex. More details, including concrete examples of the concepts described below, will follow later in the book.

> **Identity formation** The process of building, maintaining, and/or reconstructing an identity.

One approach focuses on **identity formation**, which is the process of building, maintaining, or reconstructing an identity. This approach was introduced in the 1960s when James Marcia (1966) developed the identity status interview (see Chapter 7) and distinguished between the dimensions of **commitment** and **exploration**. Commitment reflects the extent to which individuals have made choices in particular life domains and to which they engage in concrete

> **Commitment** The degree to which individuals have made choices in particular life domains and to which they engage in concrete activities to implement these choices.

> **Exploration** The process of seeking, reflecting on, and comparing potential choices before commitments are made.

activities to implement these choices. Exploration is the process of seeking for, reflecting on, and comparing potential choices of commitments.

Also important is how people deal with the complex combinations of different parts of their identity and how they present (or hide or de-emphasize) these in different contexts (Galliher et al., 2017). This process is related to the identity function of coherence and to the wide variety of identity domains that were discussed before. It is referred to as **identity negotiation** (see Chapter 9). Especially regarding identity negotiation, it is crucial to understand the societal context including characteristics related to inequality.

> **Identity negotiation** How people navigate the complex combinations of different parts of their identity and how they choose to present (or hide/de-emphasize) these in different contexts.

Less of an aspect of identity, but more of a whole approach to studying answers to the question "who are you?", is the study of **narrative identity**. It is based on the idea that we form stories about ourselves that we may or may not tell others, and that these stories can contain much information about how we see ourselves (McAdams & McLean, 2013). There are numerous ways in which such stories can be examined, and you'll be able to practice with this in Chapter 8.

> **Narrative identity** Identity represented as an autobiographical life story that we carry with us, but that evolves.

These are just a couple of the identity topics covered in the book. Other topics, which include identity capital, identity styles, identity motives, identity distress, and identity content, will be explained in later chapters to make sure this chapter doesn't get too long. Nonetheless, you should have a first idea of what is meant by "identity". The meaning of the second word that describes this book's topic, development, might seem obvious, but is also more complex than you might think.

What is development?

In everyday life the word "**development**" is often used to describe something that changes. However, development is just as often characterized by stability as we, in some ways, also remain the same person across time. Also, do you think that no longer feeling thirsty after having a sip of water qualifies as developmental change? Probably not. This might seem like a silly example of a change that obviously is not developmental, but there are changes for which it is harder to determine whether they're developmental or not. Take a change from three months of disinterest in school to a month of dedicated schoolwork. Is this a temporary thing, or is it the beginning of a whole new approach to school? That's not that easy to determine, so deciding on what counts as development isn't as straightforward as it may seem. Luckily, people called developmental scientists have defined development to provide some common ground on this complex topic. They emphasize that development is characterized by both stability and change, and that not all change is developmental. To be considered developmental, change needs to have three qualities: it needs to be organized, systematic, and successive (Johnson et al., 2024).

> **Development** What we are like across time, characterized by stability and change. For change to be developmental, it has to be organized, systematic, and successive.

Organized means the changes must represent a clear pattern that has a structure to it. It cannot just be random fluctuation. So, if in our previous example the disinterest in school returns after just a month of dedicated schoolwork, then it was just temporary and not a developmental change. It also has to be coherent. So, let's say we track the dedication of the student in our example across multiple days and it seems like their dedication on an average day may be higher in the current month than it was in previous months, but it's really going from extreme high to extreme low, then we wouldn't be able to call it a coherent change (yet). Therefore, it wouldn't be considered development.

Systematic means that the changes for one aspect of a person have to be related to some kind of change in another aspect of that same person.

Therefore, only being more dedicated to one's math class but not to other classes typically wouldn't be regarded as development. It would have to be broader ranging for that. For example, increases in commitment to education tend to have an impact on a whole range of actions that have to do with school, and therefore would be considered developmental change.

Successive means that for changes to be developmental, they must at least be partly explained by changes that occurred earlier. This can be because earlier changes may limit the immediate options for future changes, with an emphasis on immediate. In other words, it is not that once you are on a particular developmental path you're on it forever, because there's a ton of evidence against ideas like that! However, you will always carry some version of the memories of your experiences with you once you've been through certain experiences. For example, in the song "Teenage Dirtbag" by a band called Wheatus there's a line saying "he lives on my block and drives an IROC" (that's a very cool car in my opinion!). My wife thought the line said, "he lives on my block, he drives, and I walk". The reason why I bring this up is because for the foreseeable future I'll always think of her version of the lyrics when I hear the song. So, there you go: there's a bit of irreversibility in some of the changes we go through. And some of the bigger changes we go through do affect future changes.

Conclusion: Identity development

In this chapter you learned that identity is all about answers to questions like "who am I?" and "who are we?". This chapter also covered a brief introduction to the many different parts and processes involved in overall identity, and a definition of development as characterized by stability and change, including a description of what does and doesn't count as developmental change. Putting all of that together makes it clear that **identity development** concerns stability and change in how we see ourselves and think about ourselves. To speak of developmental change in identity, it needs to be organized, systematic, and successive.

> **Identity development** How we see ourselves and/or think about ourselves across time, characterized by both stability and change (see also "development").

This was a necessary introduction before we can move on to the next two chapters. In Chapter 2 it will be outlined why and how it is crucial to consider cultural context in the study of identity. Chapter 3 provides an overview of the history of the study of identity.

Further sources

1. Schwartz, S. J., Luyckx, K., & Vignoles, V. L. (2011). *Handbook of Identity Theory and Research*. Springer.

   If you want to know more about a specific identity topic, check out a handbook like this one. The chapters may sometimes be a bit challenging to read as they're often written for advanced (graduate) students and/or even professors, but you will be able to appreciate how much knowledge there is about even specific aspects of identity!

2. Obama, B. (2020). *A Promised Land*. Crown.

   This is a good example of an autobiography. It gives you an idea about how Barack Obama sees himself and his presidency. Keep in mind that you don't need to like the authors to like their autobiographies!

References

Erikson, E. H. (1950/1993). *Childhood and society*. Norton.

Erikson, E. H. (1968/1994). *Identity: Youth and crisis*. Norton.

Galliher, R. V., McLean, K. C., & Syed, M. (2017). An integrated developmental model for studying identity content in context. *Developmental Psychology, 53*, 2011–2022. https://doi.org/10.1037/dev0000299

Johnson, S. K., Klimstra, T. A., & Lerner, R. M. (2024). Concepts and theories of human development. In: Bornstein, M. H., & Lamb, M. E. (Eds.), *Developmental Science: An Advanced Textbook*. Routledge. https://doi.org/10.4324/9781003387145-2

Marcia, J. E. (1966). Development and validation of ego-identity status. *Journal of Personality and Social Psychology, 3*, 551–558. https://doi.org/10.1037/h0023281

McAdams, D. P., & McLean, K. C. (2013). Narrative identity. *Current Directions in Psychological Science, 22*, 233–238. https://doi.org/10.1177/0963721413475622

Pasupathi, M. (2014). Identity development: Dialogue between normative and pathological developmental approaches. *Journal of Personality Disorders, 28*, 113–120. https://doi.org/10.1521/pedi.2014.28.1.113

Schwartz, S. J., Luyckx, K., & Vignoles, V. L. (2011). *Handbook of Identity Theory and Research*. Springer. https://doi.org/10.1007/978-1-4419-7988-9

Umaña-Taylor, A. J. (2011). Ethnic Identity. In: Schwartz, S., Luyckx, K., & Vignoles, V. (Eds.), *Handbook of Identity Theory and Research*. Springer. https://doi.org/10.1007/978-1-4419-7988-9_33

Vignoles, V. L., Schwartz, S. J., & Luyckx, K. (2011). Introduction: Toward an integrative view of identity. In: Schwartz, S., Luyckx, K., & Vignoles, V. (Eds.), *Handbook of Identity Theory and Research*. Springer. https://doi.org/10.1007/978-1-4419-7988-9_1

Chapter 2

Identity and cultural context

Much of what the typical textbook covers on identity development is based on concepts developed, and studies conducted, in North America and Western Europe. It already is quite naïve to think that everyone within the United Kingdom, the United States, or across Western Europe shares the exact same cultural background. A straightforward example comes about when we would consider the United Kingdom one country. There would likely be few Scottish people who'd consider themselves completely the same as the English, or vice versa. Similarly, Indigenous people in Alaska, such as the Iñupiat, cannot be considered the same as Indigenous people in the South-Western United States, such as the Navajo. A good way of annoying me as a Frisian is to say I'm exactly like people from the Amsterdam area in The Netherlands. And then I haven't mentioned cultural variation within countries resulting from (historical) patterns of immigration, slavery, or displacement. In sum, there is much cultural variation within countries.

Groups that are, or have been, in close geographical proximity tend to share more similarities with each other than groups that reside in places far away from each other. This may be because they have been dealing with somewhat similar physical environments, share a common language, or have mutually intelligible languages. Therefore, it might make sense to focus on at least partly the same general aspects of identity when you only consider people within a particular geographical region. But what if we take a broader viewpoint by focusing on cultures around the world? Does it then still make sense to look at identity development across cultures in the same way? Or would that perhaps only be viable for some aspects of identity and not others? This chapter will address issues like these. First, culture will be defined. Second, an overview will be provided of some of what is known about identity development across a broader variety of cultures. In the third and final section, the focus of the rest of the book will be clarified.

What is culture?

One thing you may have heard someone say is that some people "have" culture and others don't, or that at least some people have "more" culture

DOI: 10.4324/9781003557593-3

than others. This is a misconception! We all "have" culture, it's just that for some of us our culture is more visible than for others, because the culture of the majority can become regarded as a "standard" or "normal" and therefore no longer be seen as culture. With that misconception out of the way, we can look at how scientists define culture.

There are various definitions of **culture**, with some being over 150 years old. Back then, Tylor (1871, p. 1) defined culture as ". . . that complex whole which includes knowledge, belief, art, morals, law, custom, and any other capabilities and habits acquired by man as a member of society." This is a rather inclusive definition (if we'd assume Tylor meant "humanity" with "man") as it covers a wide range of attributes. Tylor even acknowledged that there are still more than the ones he listed. Moreover, the definition emphasizes that culture is something that is acquired. Probably very few people would disagree with that, as it seems obvious that we're not born with "culture". It is something that we obtain, both through formal schooling and in informal ways through just living our life, navigating challenges and opportunities, and getting reactions from others on the things we do.

> **Culture** Acknowledging that there is a variety of definitions, it is a complex combination of knowledge, beliefs, expressions, morals, laws, customs, and other things that we acquire as members of our societies (Tylor, 1871). It is also something that is easier to see in others who are different from you, but that you may become more aware of when you encounter those differences (Agar, 1994).

More recent definitions still emphasize that culture is something you acquire but add that it is important to consider contrast. For example, Agar (1994, p. 20) noted that culture can be seen as:

> something *those* people "have", but it's more than that . . . it is also something that *happens to you* when you encounter differences, become aware of something in yourself, and work to figure out why the differences appeared. Culture is an awareness, a consciousness, one that reveals the hidden self, and opens paths to other ways of being.

According to this definition it makes perfect sense that you think that you don't have "culture" if you're part of a majority or dominant group. In addition, something like "mainstream" American culture with features like its famous fast-food chains or movie industry, may become such a dominant international standard that it's no longer seen as "culture" whereas it truly is!

Now that we have established what culture is, it becomes important to define where culture is represented and how it comes about. Rogoff (2003) emphasized the importance of **activity settings**, that is, the spaces we live our life in. She pointed to the importance of the physical and social features of those settings. To explain how this may work for physical features, think about two countries where people ride their bikes a lot: Denmark and The Netherlands. It'd be possible to assume that this is due to a genetically inherited concern about global warming and inclination to participate in physical exercise. But, sorry Danish people and fellow-Dutchies, the more likely explanation is that the bike became an important part of both cultures because Denmark and The Netherlands are among the flattest countries in the world, they're pretty small with relatively compact cities, and despite a good bunch of rainy days the temperatures typically don't get very extreme. So, it's a lot easier to use your bike than in, let's say, the steep roads of the Scottish Highlands, a suburban-sprawled city in the United States covering 200 square miles, or tropical Singapore. Similar examples can be made for social features. In some places, people talk to each other, have picnic parties open to everyone, and walk-on sports events. In other places, there may be lots of people, but they all do their own thing like listening to the music playing through their earbuds or checking social media on their phone. The former setting is a place of social connection, whereas the latter one fosters a sense of individuality. Obviously, both have pros and cons. The point is that in places where there are more activity settings characterized by social connection the culture as a whole becomes more described by connection rather than individuality. Long story short: physical and social features of activity settings matter for what cultures will be like. This can then impact what is considered important to one's identity.

Activity settings The spaces we live in, in a very general sense. These spaces have physical and social features that affect what the culture will be like.

Culture is further represented in the tools and signs we use in activity settings (Vygotsky, 1978). **Tools** include what you may have already been

Tools (as in Vygotsky's work on culture) Any physical object that humans use in the environments they live in and move through. Could include things that are widely known as tools such as hammers, but also other things like umbrellas and devices such as phones.

thinking of, so hammers, screwdrivers, and whatever else you'd find in a toolbox, but are not limited to that. The category of tools Vygotsky referred to includes any physical object that humans use in the environments they live in and move through. Sometimes these are to simply deal with environmental factors. Examples of such tools are umbrellas to deal with the rain, or just clothes to deal with low temperatures or for tempering the impact of the sun on your skin. Tools can also be means to change our environment, for example when we use pruning shears to change the shape of trees (or to avoid getting hit in the face by the same branch every time you leave the house). And yes: your phones, earbuds or headsets, and other devices you carry around are also tools. As mentioned previously, the absence or presence of such devices impact social features of the context. As a result, the way people engage with each other has changed in noticeable ways ever since mobile devices became mainstream, so since the late 1990s and early 2000s. They have also changed the ways identities are constructed and have even added identity domains such as online identities (Wängqvist & Frisén 2016).

The **signs** Vygotsky (1978) referred to are sometimes called psychological tools, as they could be perceived as tools that are not physical objects. They are things such as language, writing systems (e.g., alphabets), and number systems. These heavily affect our thoughts, emotions, and behavior. Let's take language as an example. Language is always evolving, for example evidenced by the fact that you are likely to use words or phrases when you communicate with your same-aged peers that older folks (probably including me) would be very unfamiliar with. However, those words and phrases often are important within your (sub) cultural setting. In that sense, cross-generational differences in language use reflect cultural change. If you look more internationally, there is the phenomenon that some languages which are connected to cold and snowy regions, such as Russian, contain more words and expressions for snow than, for example, the English language does (Krupnik & Müller-Wille, 2010). This suggests that environmental, in this case meteorological, features become embedded in the language as they are useful for communicating in that particular environment and the culture that goes with it. As a result of this broader phenomenon, what is identity-relevant may also differ by culture.

Signs (as in Vygotsky's work on culture) Sometimes also called psychological tools, they include things such as language, writing systems (e.g., alphabets), and number systems that shape our thinking in terms of how we remember, perceive, and behave.

Key to understanding Vygotsky's (1978) and Rogoff's (2003) views on culture is that individuals and culture are inseparable. In other words, we are not just influencing or influenced by our culture, we actually ARE our culture. To understand how that works, the concept of master narratives is relevant. **Master narratives** are defined as "culturally shared stories that provide frameworks within which individuals can locate and story their own experiences" (McLean et al., 2018, p. 633). Despite being culturally shared, master narratives aren't always directly visible to those who are part of a particular culture because they represent norms, things that are taken for granted by many people and therefore seen as "normal". An example of a master narrative in the context of the United States would be the individualistic belief that you are THE factor in determining your own success. Despite the fact that probably everyone has encountered situations with circumstances out of your control, like other people getting in the way of your success, this individualistic believe is still strongly present. In fact, it likely is spreading to other parts of the world through media.

Master narratives "culturally shared stories that provide frameworks within which individuals can locate and story their own experiences" (McLean et al., 2018, p. 633).

In The Netherlands, where I'm from and lived for much of my life, there was and largely still is a master narrative of "us" being a morally just country. This made (and makes) conversations about parts of our history that aren't "morally just" (e.g., colonialism, slave trade, and slavery) difficult. There's also a Dutch master narrative saying that everyone should be able to say whatever they want to whoever they want, and that people who get offended by that should just get over that. I don't necessarily agree with that, but it's a pretty convenient one to point to here in case there are Dutch people who don't like my reference to the not-so-morally-just parts of Dutch history . . .

Master narratives affect identities of individuals (McLean et al., 2018). Because master narratives are culturally specific, they also contribute to cultural differences in identity development. They don't just affect the course of identity development, but also what parts of our identity we are likely to express, and how we express these parts.

In sum, there is a wide variety of reasons why identity development is affected by culture. But what has been done with this knowledge? And what do we know about approaches to identity research around the world? These are the topics of the next section.

Approaches to identity research across cultures

Given the vast cultural differences there are and the psychological impact of these differences, it would make sense to study identity in a wide range of different settings. Also, it would make sense to have this be done by researchers representing a wide range of cultural backgrounds, because if we all look at the world a little differently, we would learn a lot from honoring a range of perspectives. Unfortunately, that hasn't really been the situation. What we know is not based on a universal knowledge base, but largely on a limited number of countries. Even within the countries that are typically covered, there tends to be a focus on a specific demographic: college students (Henrich et al., 2010). What adds to the problem is that college students historically haven't been all that representative of the general population in terms of, for example, race, ethnicity, and family income and wealth.

All of this would be less bad if it would be more widely acknowledged that what we know about identity largely concerns the identities of a specific group of people studied through a specific cultural lens: that of predominantly white North American or Western European identity researchers. I intentionally used "largely" and "predominantly" in the previous sentence, because there's also good news! There is research on identity in the rest of the world and some of this has been bundled since the 2010s (e.g., Adams & van de Vijver, 2022). This research can be divided into roughly two categories: studies that used an emic approach and ones that used an etic approach (Pike, 1967). Studies with an **emic** approach look at a phenomenon, in this case identity, in a culture-specific way. An example of this would be investigating what is important to a specific cultural group in answering questions like "who am I?" and "who are we?" by just simply asking them and then analyzing their responses and looking for what appears to be important to most of the members of that group. In other words, rather than assuming that their identity development is guided by the same principles that have been used to study identity development in, for example, college students from the United States, you would give research participants the opportunity to show that they approach identity development in very different ways that can't really be caught by approaches that have been used elsewhere.

Emic approach A culture-specific approach that acknowledges that basic concepts, such as identity, might have a different meaning and may therefore be expressed very differently across cultures.

> **Etic** approach An approach to cultural studies that relies on the assumption that whatever it is that is being compared across cultures, is expressed in a sufficiently similar way to make direct comparisons.

With the **etic** approach researchers do assume that whichever identity part they are studying can be examined in roughly the same way across the cultures they focus on. They may have good reasons for this as they may have used an emic approach before and found that the same aspects came up for the cultures they compared. In other words, one approach isn't necessarily better than the other and both emic and etic approaches have advantages and disadvantages. But what has been found with these approaches?

Etic approaches

In one example of the etic approach, researchers investigated whether identity dimensions of commitment and exploration that are typically used in research on college students in Western European countries work in a similar way for college students from other countries such as Poland, Romania, Türkiye, China, and Japan (Crocetti et al., 2015). That turned out to be the case in that study. The authors still emphasized that you can't just look at exploration and commitment and then, for example, say that Turkish students are more committed than Polish students as the Polish students may have been comparing themselves to other Polish students and the Turkish students may have been comparing themselves to other Turkish students. That phenomenon affects commitment and exploration scores as well! Also, although the identity dimensions included in the Crocetti et al. (2015) study may be relevant in all the included countries, there might also be culture-specific identity dimensions. Those would be ones that are relevant for describing identity development in some countries or cultures, but not in others.

Other studies with an etic approach, focusing on college students from the Northern Indian region of Ladakh (Ozer et al., 2019a, 2019b), showed that some forms of identity exploration that the researchers "imported" from studies conducted in Western Europe (i.e., Belgium) worked in a different way for Ladakh youth compared to Belgian youth. Interestingly, for Ladakh students who endorsed Western cultural values more strongly than their peers did, identity development did work in ways that were more similar to those observed in the Western part of the world. This shows that globalization, or in this case Westernization, impacts comparability of identity processes across the world, but for some youth more than for others.

You just read about a very small selection of findings obtained with etic approaches. Further research using an etic approach has been summarized elsewhere (e.g., Klimstra & Adams, 2021). The main point of this brief overview is that valuable cross-cultural comparisons can be done with an etic approach. However, etic approaches don't always work and may lead to overlooking culture-specific forms of identity development. Emic approaches, for investigating culture-specific aspects of identity development, are important to be considered as well.

Emic approaches

There is quite a lot of literature on emic approaches to identity, primarily focused on cultural identity. Cultural identity is about making choices regarding the beliefs and practices that you adopt from one or multiple cultural communities (Jensen et al., 2011). As cultures are unique, so are the identity processes related to cultural identity formation. There are helpful books that provide in-depth examples of this (e.g., Adams & van de Vijver, 2022). This section focuses on examples of unique effects of culture on identity processes beyond cultural identity.

The first example is a study conducted in Macau, China. Macau was a Portuguese colony until 1999, and therefore its culture represents a mix of Portuguese and Chinese values and customs (Ouyang et al., 2016). The study focused on vocational identity in college students. Simply put: vocational identity concerns answers to questions relevant to what kind of job you aim to get. Based on analyses of interviews, the researchers found that students in Macau often try to figure out whether their preferred options would be aligned with local norms about what a good job is. In addition, they often referred to the importance of navigating family expectations, including ones about providing financial stability. Western models of vocational identity formation typically do not include such themes. This obviously is not to say that family and societal pressures do not play a role in vocational identity formation for students in, for example, London, Geneva, or Chicago. However, researchers studying vocational identity in the Western world have typically regarded it as a personal process. Thus, an emic, or culture-specific, approach can point to aspects of identity development that would otherwise be overlooked.

The second example concerns more of a mixed emic-etic approach. The aim of this study (Arndt & Naudé, 2016) was to understand identity development of Black adolescents from different ethnic groups (primarily Sotho, Tswana, or Xhosa) in South Africa. The authors partly used an etic approach by focusing on identity concepts grounded in Western literature, such as identity continuity (see Chapter 1). Adolescents clearly indicated that aspects of individuality and uniqueness were very important in their identity development, which is similar to what has been observed in, for example, the United States and Western European countries. However, the study also used an emic approach to make sure that culture-specific approaches to identity development would also be discussed. This led to the insight that for some participating South African adolescents, uniqueness and individuality were in conflict with a desire to belong and be accepted within their community. The researchers explained that what contributed to this was their struggle to balance their community's traditions, culture, and their sense of pride of being African, with Western values, including ones related to Christianity.

Another example of a mixed emic-etic approach is a study on Japanese youth (ages 18 to 25) on the relationship between aspects of identity and well-being (Hihara et al., 2020). For the identity part, an etic approach was used as the focus was on identity commitment and exploration processes measured with a questionnaire developed in The Netherlands. However, on the well-being side the authors focused on the Japanese culture-specific phenomenon of hikikomori. Hikikomori is acute and severe social withdrawal, where people retreat into their homes or even their rooms. It started being observed in the late 1990s and is sometimes thought to be caused by rapid changes in Japanese society from more collectivistic values emphasizing the importance of the larger group, to more individualistic values emphasizing the importance of the individual. Japan's economic depression and changes to the job market made it harder to enter adult social roles such as full-time jobs, which may have further contributed to the rise of hikikomori. Hihara et al. (2020) found that Japanese youth whose identities were described as "diffused" (they weren't very committed and didn't do much exploration), were more likely to have more hikikomori symptoms.

The focus of this book

In sum, we know that identity development doesn't always work in the same way across cultures. However, most studies that are published in English, even many of the ones that are conducted outside of the Western world by researchers from outside the Western world, use etic approaches. In other words, the use of approaches to identity that were initially developed in countries such as Belgium, The Netherlands, and the United States is common across the world. It is important to focus on culture-specific forms of identity, or how identity relates to culture-specific phenomena, but there are a lot of cultures around the world. Unfortunately, it simply is not feasible to cover all of that in a nuanced way. Therefore, this book takes a pragmatic approach primarily focusing on the kind of research on identity development that originated in North America and Western Europe.

The goal of this chapter was to make you aware of the fact that much of the research on identity development up till now has been conducted by people from a small part of the world and usually described identity development of people from that same small part of the world. And within that small part of the world, the research hasn't been all that inclusive either, neither regarding the people who conducted it, nor regarding the people who were studied. This book will contain reminders about that, but also keep this in mind yourself as you read this book. What you read may apply to you and those around you, but not all of it necessarily applies to everyone everywhere. Several issues pointed to in this chapter also apply to the next chapter, where an overview of the history of the study of identity development will be provided.

Further sources

1. Adams, B. G., & van de Vijver, F. J. (2022). *Non-western identity: Research and perspectives.* Springer.

   It is a more advanced book, so it might sometimes be a bit harder to follow, but it does give you a great idea of how identity is approached in countries outside of the Western world.

2. Namibia Up (see https://www.namibiaup.com/home).

   This is the website of a film featuring 18-year-old Namibians. A university professor was heavily involved in the making of this award-winning documentary film. By the time I wrote this, you could only see the trailers, but check the website for lots of information, screenings, and trailers. Given the age range and setting, you will be able to see how youth in Namibia deal with identity issues.

References

Adams, B. G., & van de Vijver, F. J. (2022). *Non-western identity: Research and perspectives.* Springer. https://doi.org/10.1007/978-3-030-77242-0

Agar, M. (1994). *Language shock. understanding the culture of conversation.* William Morrow.

Arndt, N., & Naudé, L. (2016). Contrast and contradiction: Being a Black adolescent in contemporary South Africa. *Journal of Psychology in Africa, 26*, 267–275. https://doi.org/10.1080/14330237.2016.1185913

Crocetti, E., Cieciuch, J., Gao, C.-H., Klimstra, T., Lin, C.-L., Matos, P. M., Morsünbül, Ü., Negru, O., Sugimura, K., Zimmermann, G., & Meeus, W. (2015). National and gender measurement invariance of the Utrecht-Management of Identity Commitments Scale (U-MICS): A 10-nation study with university students. *Assessment, 22*(6), 753–768. https://doi.org/10.1177/1073191115584969

Henrich, J., Heine, S. J., & Norenzayan, A. (2010). The weirdest people in the world? *Behavioral and Brain Sciences, 33*, 61–83. https://doi.org/10.1017/S0140525X0999152X

Hihara, S., Ishibashi, I., Umemura, T., & Sugimura, K. (2020). Roles of configurations of multiple identity domains in adaptive and maladaptive functioning in Japanese emerging adults: Using a culturally relevant index. *Emerging Adulthood, 8*, 373–381. https://doi.org/10.1177/2167696819858457

Jensen, L. A., Arnett, J. J., & McKenzie, J. (2011). Globalization and cultural identity. In: Schwartz, S., Luyckx, K., & Vignoles, V. (Eds.), *Handbook of Identity Theory and Research*. Springer. https://doi.org/10.1007/978-1-4419-7988-9_13

Klimstra, T. A., & Adams, B. G. (2021). Perspectives on personal identity development in Western and Non-Western contexts. In: Adams, B. G., & van de Vijver, F. J. R. (Eds.), *Non-Western Identity. Identity in a Changing World*. Springer. https://doi.org/10.1007/978-3-030-77242-0_13

Krupnik, I., & Müller-Wille, L. (2010). Franz Boas and Inuktitut Terminology for Ice and Snow: From the Emergence of the Field to the "Great Eskimo Vocabulary Hoax". In: Krupnik, I., Aporta, C., Gearheard, S., Laidler, G., & Kielsen Holm, L. (Eds.). *SIKU: Knowing Our Ice*. Springer. https://doi.org/10.1007/978-90-481-8587-0_16

McLean, K. C., Lilgendahl, J. P., Fordham, C., Alpert, E., Marsden, E., Szymanowski, K., & McAdams, D. P. (2018). Identity development in cultural context: The role of deviating from master narratives. *Journal of Personality, 86*, 631–651. https://doi.org/10.1111/jopy.12341

Ouyang, B., Jin, S. R., & Tien, H. L. S. (2016). Vocational identity formation of college students in Macau. *The Career Development Quarterly, 64*, 244–258. https://doi.org/10.1002/cdq.12058

Ozer, S., Meca, A., & Schwartz, S. J. (2019a). Globalization and identity development among emerging adults from Ladakh. *Cultural Diversity & Ethnic Minority Psychology, 25*, 515–526. https://doi.org/10.1037/cdp0000261

Ozer, S., Meca, A., & Schwartz, S. J. (2019b). Identity processes in Ladakhi emerging adults: Testing the dimensions of identity development scale in an Indigenous Himalayan population. *Emerging Adulthood, 7*, 45–51. https://doi.org/10.1177/2167696818754919

Pike, K. L. (1967). *Language in relation to a unified theory of structure of human behavior* (2nd ed.). Mouton.

Rogoff, B. (2003). *The cultural nature of human development*. Oxford University Press.

Tylor, E. (1871). *Primitive Culture: Research into the Development of Mythology, Philosophy, Religion, Art and Custom*. Putnam.

Vygotsky, L. S. (1978). *Mind in society: Development of higher psychological processes* (M. Cole, V. Jolm-Steiner, S. Scribner, & E. Souberman, Eds.). Harvard University Press. https://doi.org/10.2307/j.ctvjf9vz4

Wängqvist, M., & Frisén, A. (2016). Who am I online? Understanding the meaning of online contexts for identity development. *Adolescent Research Review, 1*, 139–151. https://doi.org/10.1007/s40894-016-0025-0Glossary

Chapter 3

A brief history of the study of identity

The question "who am I" is very old. Thus, people have been thinking about identity for a long time and there is no truly fair way to determine who really started the study of identity development. Claims about the history of identity dating back to ancient Greece likely are oversimplified and therefore problematic (Bamberg & Dege, 2021), but philosophers who lived during the Enlightenment period (17th and 18th century) certainly laid the foundations for later research on identity development. Among these philosophers were David Hume, Immanuel Kant, and Jean Jacques Rousseau. Take for example Kant: he discussed identity as related to unity of consciousness, continuity, and as contributing to agency (feeling like you have power, or influence). This has quite some similarities to the three functions of coherence, continuity, and distinctiveness, discussed in Chapter 1! This chapter cannot discuss all the nuances in the writings of these and other philosophers who wrote about identity(-like) concepts. An important thing to remember, though, is that "starting points" of the study of a certain concept are always debatable. Also, as creative and brilliant as we all may be, when we think of something "new" someone else has probably already thought of something similar at some point in history. Getting recognized as a founder of a field often is just a matter of saying, or writing, the right thing to the right audience at the right moment in time. Keep this in mind when the history of research in identity development is discussed in this chapter.

The question "who are we", relevant to understanding group identities, is likely equally old, but its recent history, within the previous and current century, is largely separated from that of the "who am I" question. Although predated by early 20th century work on in-group versus out-group thinking (Sumner, 1906), most commonly the formulation of social identity theory (Tajfel & Turner, 1986) is considered a key point in the history of the study of group identities. Social identity theory focuses on people's knowledge of them (or us, if you will) being part of certain social groups, and that this group membership has some emotional significance and may be related to people's values. Thus, concepts such as

DOI: 10.4324/9781003557593-4

ethnic identity, national identity, and gender identity would all usually be considered social identities. Because identity development is so broad we will again have to focus and are going to zoom in on the parts of identity that historically have been of most interest to developmental scientists: personal identity, or as I've been calling it informally, the study of "who am I" questions.

The early times

The moment that Wilhelm Wundt opened his experimental psychology lab in Leipzig, Germany, in 1879 is usually considered the starting point of psychology as a scientific discipline. Around the same time, William James had started teaching psychology classes on the other side of the Atlantic Ocean at Harvard University. Whereas Wundt had very broad interests, likely including questions of the "who am I" kind, James's work on these kinds of questions is widely known and is still at the basis of current work relevant to the study of identity development. What James's work was about is the self, or more specifically the "I" and the "me".

The "me", or the self as known, contains everything a person can call theirs, which includes their experiences (James, 1910). Later work on **possible selves** is grounded in this part of James's writings, and so is the concept of **self-esteem**. Possible selves have been described as "the elements of the self-concept that represent the individual's goals, motives, fears, and anxieties" and as "specific and vivid senses, images, or conceptions of oneself in future states and circumstances" (Oyserman & Markus, 1990, p. 113). In other words, they could be described as answers to questions such as "who would I like to be" and "who would I try to avoid becoming", and hence can motivate people to develop their identity in a certain direction (Dunkel & Anthis, 2001). Self-esteem is an individual's own evaluation of their worth as a person (Orth & Robins, 2014) and therefore also highly relevant to people's sense of identity and the development thereof. Thus, parts of the

Possible selves "The elements of the self-concept that represent the individual's goals, motives, fears, and anxieties" and "specific and vivid senses, images, or conceptions of oneself in future states and circumstances" (Oyserman & Markus, 1990, p. 113).

Self-esteem An individual's own evaluation of their worth as a person.

"me" are certainly important to identity development but may not quite represent how we see identity nowadays.

The "I", or the self as knower, gets to a more abstract level. James described it as that part of us that is conscious (or aware) also about there being a "me" (James, 1910). It's the "I" that helps us make sense of there not just being one "me" or one "self", but that all these "me's" and "selves" are part of the same "I". That awareness provides a sense of continuity, or a feeling that who you were in the past is linked to who you are in the present and who you will be in the future. So, the "I" has obvious linkages to the continuity function of identity discussed in Chapter 1. In addition, it is also linked to the coherence function (making sense of the puzzle of the different parts of who we are) discussed there. Given that James (1910) formulated the "I" as a passing state and as something very abstract, he felt like it wasn't something that was suitable for scientific inquiry. However, the identity concepts covered in the rest of this chapter and other chapters in this book do share some similarities with what James (1910) described as the "I".

Id In Freud's theory, id contained energies that come from unconscious instinctual drives.

Ego In Freud's theory, the ego regulates the instinctual drives of the id based on the standards set by the superego.

Superego In Freud's theory, this represents ideals to work towards based on what people perceive to be standards set by authority figures or society more broadly.

There is another rather (in)famous person whose work was foundational for the study of identity development as we know it now: Sigmund Freud. Although much of his work is considered controversial by now, a substantial portion of his work still has value even if it's at a more abstract theoretical level. One such part concerns his writing on **id**, **ego**, and **superego** (Lapsley & Stey, 2012). The id was described as containing energies that come from unconscious instinctual drives. The superego represents an ideal to work towards based on people's perceptions of the standards set by their parents or caregivers, and later by society more broadly. The ego is thought to "negotiate" between the superego and the id: it regulates the instinctual drives of the id based on the standards set by the superego. In other words, the ego is responsible for regulating our behaviour, cognitions, and emotions to fit the reality of our social environment. According to this idea, the ego sometimes strikes a perfect balance. However, it can also overdo it on the regulatory functions and suppress inner needs too much, causing people to live with external standards too much in mind, or, conversely, it can not suppress enough of the instinctual drive, thereby causing problems for individuals to function in society.

At this point Freudian theory may not seem relevant to identity development, but it is! What is now referred to as identity formation stems from something originally called ego identity. More importantly, the person who came up with the concept of ego identity and is seen as the founder of modern-day research on identity was heavily influenced by Sigmund Freud and trained by his daughter Anna Freud. The name of this person was Erik H. Erikson.

The 1950s: Erikson's initial work on identity

In 1950, Erikson (1950/1993) wrote his book *Childhood and Society* which famously divided the lifespan into eight developmental stages that all come with a developmental task (for a detailed discussion see Chapter 4). What makes it a key point in the history of the study on identity development is that Erikson provided a definition of identity that is still highly influential (see Chapter 1). He described adolescence, covering roughly the period from age 12 to 18, as crucial for developing a sense of identity as opposed to role confusion. It is important to remember that this theorizing of Erikson is widely perceived as the foundation of the study of identity as we know it today.

The 1960s and 1970s: Further contributions by Erikson and the introduction of the identity status approach

In *Childhood and Society* (Erikson, 1950/1993), identity versus role confusion is just one of the eight developmental tasks despite it being depicted as an important one. However, in the 1960s Erikson elaborated on his ideas on identity which led to the publication of a book entirely dedicated to it. This book was titled *Identity: Youth and Crisis* (Erikson, 1968/1994). It is that book that inspired identity research for years to come. Many ideas outlined are still relevant today! Examples of this are the concept of an identity crisis, which you likely are familiar with, and ideas on the importance of cultural influences on identity, which were particularly revolutionary at that time. Yet, Erikson's ideas were often thought to be too broad to be directly tested in research.

This issue was also addressed in the late 1960s, when James Marcia (1966) introduced the identity status approach, which got very popular in research on identity development and is still used today. Based on amounts of commitment and exploration (see Chapter 1) and how those commitments were formed (see Chapter 5), he classified individuals into so-called **identity statuses**. An example of an identity status is moratorium, which basically represents Erikson's (1968/1994) concept of identity crisis. It reflects a state in which a person has weak commitment but is exploring a lot. If you're trying to figure out what to major in, or if you gather information and opinions to decide on whether you want to do a master's program or work for a couple of years and you haven't really settled on anything yet, you might be in this status. In Chapter 5, you'll learn that being in a moratorium status is not necessarily a bad thing. Other identity statuses will be discussed there, too.

> **Identity statuses** A classification scheme to describe what an individual's identity is like in terms of commitment and exploration at a particular moment.

The 1980s: Refining and rethinking identity research and the introduction of the narrative approach

Despite, or perhaps because of, its popularity, the identity status approach started attracting some critique in the 1980s. Such critiques pointed out that the approach falls short in explaining how people get to a particular identity status (Bosma, 1985). Also, both commitment and exploration were considered too broad, and it was pointed out that there were multiple ways to explore and be committed (e.g., Bosma, 1985; Grotevant, 1987). These critiques immediately affected how the identity statuses and underlying dimensions were interpreted, and later led to new models of identity formation. For example, Berzonsky (1989) introduced the identity styles approach to describe and explain individual differences in how people typically approach identity-related questions. For example, people with one of these styles, the normative style, tend to make identity-relevant decisions based on what they think are norms and standards upheld by others important to them. For example, they may prioritize their caregivers' wishes and desires over their own when choosing a major in college. The identity styles approach provided a first major addition to Marcia's identity status approach, and it linked identity work to theories on other concepts such as cognitive development. As there are two more styles in addition to the normative style and there's more to say about the theory behind the identity styles, the identity styles approach will be covered in more detail in Chapter 5.

The 1980s also saw the introduction of the currently popular narrative identity approach. Grounded in Erikson's (1950/1993, 1968/1994) work but not in Marcia's (1966) work, key to this approach is the idea that people's identities can be studied through analyzing (parts of) their life stories. The narrative identity approach doesn't just draw from Erikson's work but is also based on older ideas in personality psychology dating back to the 1930s (McAdams, 2011). Specifically, personology is key to narrative identity theory. Personology emphasizes the importance of motives (Murray, 1938). These could for example be related to people's need for achievement, which is where your sense of satisfaction after completing a task may come from, or the need for belongingness, which you may feel in the form of an urge to see your friends and do fun stuff together after you haven't been able to see them for a while. Such motives can be detected in the stories people tell about their lives.

For a long time, people's life stories were seen as entertaining but mostly useless for scientific research. That has changed! Stories mostly regained their popularity (Freudians had been interested in life stories, too) in the 1970s and 1980s, because of a growing recognition of the importance of memories including those about important moments or periods in our life. Such memories are called autobiographical memories. In the 1970s, Tomkins (1979; see also Singer, 1975) began to demonstrate that those autobiographical memories are organized, that people's feelings related to different parts of the memory are important, and that these organized memories and the feelings associated with them tell us important information about people's thinking patterns. Several philosophers of the same era further contributed to the interest in narratives by pointing to their importance in providing people with a sense of sameness and continuity across time (McAdams, 2011). McAdams (1985) took it one step further, arguing that identity itself could be seen as a life story, and therefore he typically is credited as the founder of narrative identity research. A narrative identity is thought of as story that we carry with us, but that evolves. Much like a play, it has characters, different plots, and scenes.

There is a lot of information in people's life stories, which is why researchers typically look for specific elements. An example of this is the presence of agency (does the person seem to think they had power to influence the situation they described?), but there are many more things! In Chapter 8, you will get to know more about this approach, and you will also get to apply it to your own life story or those of others, after you learn what kind of questions are asked to even get information on life stories. From a historical viewpoint, it is important to remember that the narrative approach has become prominent in research on identity since the 1980s.

The 1990s: Growing emphasis on the importance of context and an organization for the study of identity

Obviously, there is more to identity development than just exploration and commitment, and identity development is not going to be the same under all circumstances. Put differently: we don't all start out from the same point on any of our developmental journeys and identity development is no exception to this general rule. Although Erikson (1950/1993) had already pointed this out, a series of theories that were formulated since the 1980s but especially since the 1990s directly and specifically acknowledged this.

> **Identity capital model** A theoretical model describing a sense of identity as a resource (or "capital") that is used to navigate life. It draws from other resources, which include characteristics such as self-esteem but also factors that are unequally distributed across social classes such as financial resources.

One of these is the **identity capital model**. According to this model, a sense of identity can be seen as a resource (or "capital") in navigating life (Côté, 1996, 2002). It is "fed" by other resources, which include personality-like characteristics but also factors that are unequally distributed across social classes such as financial resources. The benefits of those resources for identity development are larger in some contexts than in others, though. The model will be further explained in Chapter 4. Somewhat similar in emphasizing the role of social and societal context, but also different in pointing out that individuals also affect their environment, are theories such as the phenomenological variant of ecological systems theory (PVEST; Spencer et al., 1997). Theories such as these can highlight the role of systemic inequalities, in the case of PVEST especially those related to race.

For any field of study, a historical marker is the founding of a society so that conferences can be organized and people with the same interests can meet each other. For the study of identity and its development, this happened in the early 1990s. After an initial meeting in 1994 in San Diego, California, the first official conference of what was then called the Society of Research on Identity Formation (SRIF) took place in 1995 on Dog Island in Florida. Renamed the International Society for Research on Identity (ISRI) in the 2010s, it is a thriving organization that still hosts conferences. If you are interested in everything identity after reading this book or hope to meet someone who can explain things in a better or different way than I do, you are encouraged to attend an ISRI conference! You certainly wouldn't be the first, or only, (undergraduate) student to do so.

The 2000s: A dedicated journal and dual-cycle models of identity development

The decade, and millennium (Y2K, as us millennials liked to call it), started with another milestone for the study of identity and its development as the field got its own dedicated scientific journal in 2001. Titled *Identity: An International Journal of Theory and Research*, it has served as a place for identity scientists to put their ideas out into the world. Identity researchers have also been publishing scientific articles in journals that serve a more general audience of psychologists and developmental scientists. However, having a specific identity journal allowed for more in-depth discussions and issues that are of more interest to identity researchers than to others. An example of this is the discussion of the impact of Erikson's *Identity: Youth and Crisis* 50 years after it was published (Schachter & Galliher, 2018).

Based on the previously mentioned critiques in the 1980s, some adjustments to Marcia's (1966) ideas on identity exploration were made by Bosma (1985) and Meeus (1996). They emphasized that exploration could also be about evaluating existing commitments even without necessarily wanting to replace those. More drastic change happened around 2008 when new identity measures were introduced that allowed identity development to be understood as a process that involves moving back and forth between two cycles. These two cycles are a formation cycle in which people construct a new (part of their) identity and an evaluation, or maintenance, cycle in which people reflect on (parts of) their current identity in a variety of ways (Crocetti, 2017). People are thought to continuously move back and forth between such cycles. These dual-cycle models of identity development will be discussed in more detail in Chapter 5 and the associated measures are discussed in Chapter 7. For now, it is important to know that after their introduction in the 2000s, much of the research in the 2010s and 2020s relied on these dual-cycle models.

Developments since 2010

The overview provided in this chapter covers broad developments over the years. Less-widely used approaches to study the development of identity were not mentioned, and that's not because they're not important!

In fact, some of those approaches will still be covered in other chapters (e.g., the dynamic systems approach in Chapter 4, identity motives in Chapter 5, and approaches emphasizing the role of social interactions in Chapter 6). Recently, defined here as since 2010, there have been several additional developments in the field.

First, the role of identity development in the development of personality pathology, so conditions such as borderline, narcissistic, and antisocial personality disorder, has become much more of a focus. Several of the people who founded the field, such as Erikson and Marcia, partly studied identity development to better understand their clients, but little of their work and that of those who followed in their footsteps focused specifically on personality disorders. Instead, their focus was more often on symptoms of depression and anxiety. There is even work focusing on anxiety-like distress specific to identity-relevant decisions such as those related to choosing a career (Berman & Weems, 2016)! The role of identity in personality pathology became a prominent area of interest when a new version of a widely used diagnostic system came out: the fifth version of the Diagnostic and Statistical Manual of Mental Disorders (DSM-5; American Psychiatric Association, 2013). DSM-5 mentioned identity disturbances as an important factor for diagnosing personality disorders, which contributed to interest in how the development of these two are related as there are numerous reasons to believe they are (e.g., Shiner et al., 2021). More about this will be covered in Chapter 6.

With the increasing popularity of the narrative approach to identity, more researchers now also combine narratives with assessments of identity dimensions such as commitment and exploration. The first of such studies already appeared before 2010 (McLean & Pratt, 2006), but since the 2010s such work, or really any work that is adopting multiple approaches to identity, is becoming more common. Perhaps this is because the generation of researchers who developed different identity concepts originally (sometimes) did so because they didn't agree with whatever identity concepts were already around, sometimes for ideological reasons. The current generation of researchers may feel less constricted by such reasons.

Along with a growing interest in narrative identity, the related master narrative framework that was discussed in Chapter 2 has also become much more widely used. As master narratives represent culturally shared stories and ideas that provide guidelines for how to tell our own personal stories (McLean et al., 2018), they can also help to clarify how systems within a particular society can influence identity development. Thus, the master narrative framework is another tool, along with the perspectives developed in the 1990s, to better understand and account for societal impacts on identity development.

Also, a variety of researchers started taking advantage of the internet (whenever someone writes "the internet" you know they didn't grow up with it . . .) and smartphone technology to track changes in identity from day to day, or even several times a day. Again, there were early examples of this from before 2010 (e.g., Yip & Fuligni, 2002), but the approach has become more widespread due to technological advances. This approach has been used for a variety of reasons, for example to examine how people express their identities in the moment, but also to show that daily events and emotions can affect identity (Sugimura & Kunnen, 2022). Somewhat related to this in that it also requires complex technology, some identity researchers have taken a more biological approach. For example, they examined the relationship between identity development and the structure of brain areas (Becht et al., 2018).

Conclusion

In sum, identity and its development have been of interest to people for many centuries but only started to be studied more systematically since the 1950s and 1960s. Many ways to approach identity and its development have been established over the years since then, and we continue to find new approaches to the interesting question of "who am I?". Now that you know a little bit about the roots of what we know about identity development, we can go more in depth on the theories in the next sections of the book!

Further sources

1. Website of the International Society for Research on Identity (ISRI); http://identityisri.org/

   If you're interested in knowing more about the people who study identity and contributed to much of what you read in this book, consider going to the website of the society that organizes conferences on this topic. You're always welcome to come to the conference!

2. Erik H. Erikson: A Life's Work; https://www.imdb.com/title/tt1925423/

   Want to know more about one of the founders of research on identity development? Then this 1992 film, published when Erikson was still alive(!), may be interesting.

References

American Psychiatric Association (2013). *Diagnostic and statistical manual of mental disorders.* (5th ed.). https://doi.org/10.1176/appi.books.9780890425596

Bamberg, M., & Dege, M. (2021). Decentering Histories of Identity. In: Bamberg, M., Demuth, C., & Watzlawik, M. (Eds.), *The Cambridge Handbook of Identity* (pp. 25–56). Cambridge University Press.

Becht, A. I., Bos, M. G., Nelemans, S. A., Peters, S., Vollebergh, W. A., Branje, S. J., . . . & Crone, E. A. (2018). Goal-directed correlates and neurobiological underpinnings of adolescent identity: A multimethod multisample longitudinal approach. *Child Development, 89*, 823–836. https://doi.org/10.1111/cdev.13048

Berman, S. L., & Weems, C. F. (2016). Identity Distress. In: Levesque, R. (Ed.), *Encyclopedia of Adolescence*. Springer. https://doi.org/10.1007/978-3-319-32132-5_143-2

Berzonsky, M. D. (1989). Identity style: Conceptualization and measurement. *Journal of Adolescent Research, 4*, 268–282. https://doi.org/10.1177/074355488943002

Bosma, H. A. (1985). *Identity development in adolescents: Coping with commitments*. Unpublished doctoral dissertation, University of Groningen, The Netherlands.

Côté, J. E. (1996). Sociological perspectives on identity formation: The culture–identity link and identity capital. *Journal of Adolescence, 19*, 417–428. https://doi.org/10.1006/jado.1996.0040

Côté, J. E. (2002). The role of identity capital in the transition to adulthood: The individualization thesis examined. *Journal of Youth Studies, 5*, 117–134. https://doi.org/10.1080/13676260220134403

Crocetti, E. (2017). Identity formation in adolescence: The dynamic of forming and consolidating identity commitments. *Child Development Perspectives, 11*, 145–150. https://doi.org/10.1111/cdep.12226

Dunkel, C., & Anthis, K. (2001). The role of possible selves in identity formation: A short-term longitudinal study. *Journal of Adolescence, 24*, 765–776. https://doi.org/10.1006/jado.2001.0433

Erikson, E. H. (1950/1993). *Childhood and society*. Norton.

Erikson, E. H. (1968/1994). *Identity: Youth and crisis*. Norton.

Grotevant, H. D. (1987). Toward a process model of identity formation. *Journal of Adolescent Research, 2*, 203–222. https://doi.org/10.1177/074355488723003

James, W. (1910). *Psychology: The briefer course*. Holt.

Lapsley, D. K., & Stey, P. C. (2012). Id, ego, superego. In: Ramachandran, V.S. (Ed.), *Encyclopedia of human behavior* (2nd ed., pp. 393–399). Academic Press/Elsevier. https://doi.org/10.1016/B978-0-12-375000-6.00199-3Marcia, J. E. (1966). Development and validation of ego-identity status. *Journal of Personality and Social Psychology, 3*, 551–558. https://doi.org/10.1037/h0023281

McAdams, D. P. (1985). *Power, intimacy, and the life story: Personological inquiries into identity*. Guilford Press.

McAdams, D. P. (2011). Narrative Identity. In: Schwartz, S., Luyckx, K., & Vignoles, V. (Eds.), *Handbook of Identity Theory and Research*. Springer. https://doi.org/10.1007/978-1-4419-7988-9_5

McLean, K. C., Lilgendahl, J. P., Fordham, C., Alpert, E., Marsden, E., Szymanowski, K., & McAdams, D. P. (2018). Identity development in

cultural context: The role of deviating from master narratives. *Journal of Personality, 86*, 631–651. https://doi.org/10.1111/jopy.12341
McLean, K. C., & Pratt, M. W. (2006). Life's little (and big) lessons: Identity statuses and meaning-making in the turning point narratives of emerging adults. *Developmental Psychology, 42*, 714–722. https://doi.org/10.1037/0012-1649.42.4.714
Meeus, W. (1996). Studies on identity development in adolescence: An overview of research and some new data. *Journal of Youth and Adolescence, 25*, 569–598.
Murray, H. A. (1938). *Explorations in personality.* Oxford University Press.
Orth, U., & Robins, R. W. (2014). The development of self-esteem. *Current Directions in Psychological Science, 23*, 381–387. https://doi.org/10.1177/0963721414547414
Oyserman, D., & Markus, H. R. (1990). Possible selves and delinquency. *Journal of Personality and Social Psychology, 59*, 112–125. https://doi.org/10.1037//0022-3514.59.1.112
Schachter, E. P., & Galliher, R. V. (2018). Fifty years since "Identity: Youth and Crisis": A renewed look at Erikson's writings on identity. *Identity, 18*, 247–250. https://doi.org/10.1080/15283488.2018.1529267
Shiner, R. L., Klimstra, T. A., Denissen, J. J., & See, A. Y. (2021). The development of narrative identity and the emergence of personality disorders in adolescence. *Current Opinion in Psychology, 37*, 49–53. https://doi.org/10.1016/j.copsyc.2020.07.024
Singer, J. L. (1975). Navigating the stream of consciousness: Research in daydreaming and related inner experience. *American Psychologist, 30*, 727–738. https://doi.org/10.1037/h0076928
Spencer, M. B., Dupree, D., & Hartmann, T. (1997). A Phenomenological Variant of Ecological Systems Theory (PVEST): A self-organization perspective in context. *Development and Psychopathology, 9*, 817–833. https://doi.org/10.1017/S0954579497001454
Sugimura, K., & Kunnen, E. S. (2022). Real-time identity processes: Empirical applications. *Identity, 22*, 1–5. https://doi.org/10.1080/15283488.2022.2036929
Sumner, W. G. (1906). *Folkways: A Study of the Sociological Importance of Usages, Manners, Customs, Mores, and Morals.* Ginn.
Tajfel, H., & Turner, J. C. (1986). The social identity theory of intergroup behavior. In: Worchel, S. & Austin, W. G. (Eds.), *The Psychology of Intergroup Behavior* (pp. 7–24). Nelson Hall.
Tomkins, S. S. (1979). Script theory: Differential magnification of affects. In: Howe, H. E. & Dienstbier, R. A. (Eds.), *Nebraska symposium on motivation* (Vol. 26, pp. 201–236). University of Nebraska Press.
Yip, T., & Fuligni, A. J. (2002). Daily variation in ethnic identity, ethnic behaviors, and psychological well–being among American adolescents of Chinese descent. *Child development, 73*, 1557–1572. https://doi.org/10.1111/1467-8624.00490

Section 2

Key theories

By the end of this section, you will:

- Understand that there are different types of theories.
- Understand what the major theories on identity development are and what they entail.
- Know how the different theories relate to each other.
- Be able to explain important theories on identity development in your own words.

DOI: 10.4324/9781003557593-5

Chapter 4

Explaining general patterns of identity development

Broad theories

Identity and its development are complicated. There are a whole lot of possible ways it may work. Before starting to test how something works, you first need to define what you're looking for. For that, you can use the definitions of identity, development, and identity development in Chapter 1. Those definitions didn't just come out of nowhere, they were based on theories. But theories go beyond definitions, or the "what". They also contain ideas on the "how", "when", and "why" of, in this case, identity development. In this chapter, broad theories on identity development will be covered. These include Erikson's theory on lifespan development and identity, McAdams's theory on personality development in which narrative identity plays an important role, dynamic systems theory, and theorizing on the role of systemic factors that affect identity development. Before moving into all of that, we'll first see what makes something a theory and what different kinds of theories can be distinguished. In other words, we'll start off with some theory on theories.

What is a theory and are all theories alike?

Let's say you're with a friend at a train station waiting for a delayed train. When you discuss possible explanations for why the train is late, you may say "my theory is that there were some sheep running on the tracks and the train had to wait for them to leave the tracks". Your friend may say "my theory is that they first forgot to schedule a train driver and then had to call someone who still had to come to the station and therefore the train left too late". But would these really be considered theories in the sciences? The answer is "not really". These statements would most likely be referred to as hypotheses, which are testable predictions about how to explain a particular phenomenon, or about how two or more variables are related (Creswell & Creswell, 2022).

DOI: 10.4324/9781003557593-6

Theory A theory can be described as "... a system of statements that integrates existing information and leads to the generation of new information" (Lerner, 2018, p. 2).

A **theory** is broader and more comprehensive than a hypothesis. It can be defined as "... a system of statements that integrates existing information and leads to the generation of new information" (Lerner, 2018, p. 2). In other words, you'd need to elaborate a good bit more on the cause of the train delay and, perhaps even more importantly, get to something that could explain more than just one train delay. Generally, theories are there to organize information, which is also referred to as data. Data can take the form of anything that can be perceived or communicated, for example it can come in the form of numbers, words, and observations. As discussing every single data point (e.g., every number) one by one is not very efficient, there are theories that can integrate data. But how do theories generate new data? Think of the definitions of identity discussed in Chapter 1. Before identity was defined, it wasn't possible to collect data on it because people wouldn't know where to start. Because there are now theories on what matters for what identity is and also about how and why it develops, we also know what kind of data to gather to study identity development.

However, not all theories are alike. Some have broad implications, even ranging into how researchers perceive "truth". Those would be called metatheories, so theories about theories, or paradigms (Lerner, 2018). Others are designed to explain more specific phenomena. Not quite as specific as a single train delay, but they could be as specific as explaining delays of trains coming into Boston's North Station, London's Saint Pancras Station, Station Feanwâlden, or whatever station you're interested in. Variation in the functions and goals of theories in terms of their breadth can be represented with a funnel, with broader and more narrow theories (Lerner, 2018). Often, and the study of identity is no exception to that, more narrow theories are related to broader theories.

In addition to some theories being broader and others more specific, there are also historical linkages between theories. One could say that newer theories often branch off from older theories, which is no coincidence because a good scientist reads the work of those who came before them. This section of the book will not take a historical approach, but the historical linkages between the broadest and mid-range theories on identity (the ones discussed in this chapter and Chapter 5) are included in Figure 4.1.

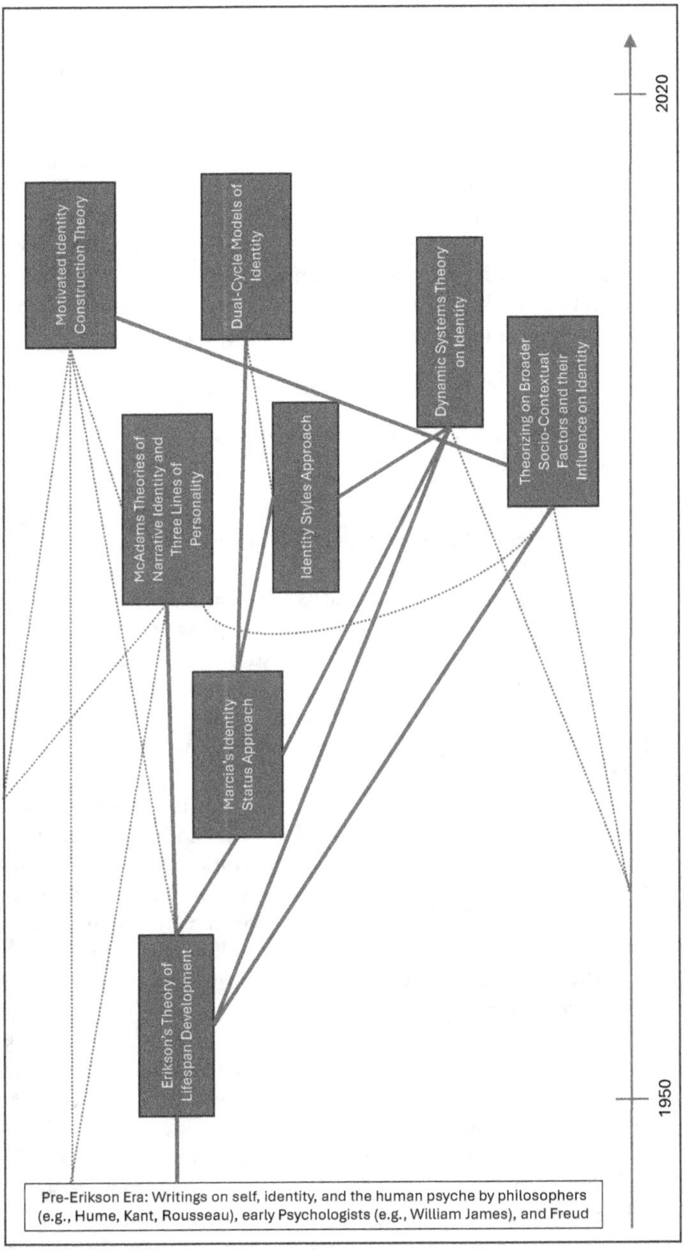

Figure 4.1 Theories of identity from a historical perspective

Instead of following a historical approach, this section of the book follows the logic of the funnel. Chapter 6 will cover the "narrowest" theories at the bottom of the funnel. Often these aren't complete theories but better described as theoretical principes. These can be used to explain phenomena in specific contexts or related to specific subtopics. Chapter 5 covers mid-range theories that have somewhat broader implications and explain broad aspects of identity development, but not the full picture. The broadest theories on identity development are Erikson's theory of lifespan development, McAdams's theory on personality development which focuses on narrative identity, a dynamic systems approach to identity, and theoretical work emphasizing the importance of systemic factors. These will be covered in the remainder of this chapter.

Erikson's theory of lifespan development and identity

In his theory on lifespan development, Erikson distinguished eight developmental stages. The first stage runs from age 0 to about 18 months and its optimal outcome is that the child develops a sense of basic trust as opposed to mistrust towards their caregivers. The optimal outcome for the final stage, which spans the last phase of life, is a sense of ego integrity as opposed to despair. Less straightforward than trust, ego integrity is about having adapted ". . . to the triumphs and disappointments adherent to being" and a sense of having been ". . . the originator of others or the generator of products and ideas" (Erikson, 1950/1993, p. 268).

Stage theory A type of developmental theory, such as Erikson's theory on lifespan development, based on the idea that there are distinct phases or steps in development.

A first common misconception about Erikson's **stage theory** that needs to be addressed is the idea that all possible work on a developmental task has to occur in the designated stage. That is not what Erikson (1950/1993) wrote! The stages only represent when particular developmental tasks, such as developing a sense of basic trust, are considered the most important. What happens before and after the life stages in which a task is central still affects the virtue to be acquired. So, according to Erikson's theory our sense of basic trust can change well after 18 months of age, and ego integrity may start developing well before the last years of our lives. Erikson did suggest that the result of one developmental task affects the resolution of the next developmental task. So, if a sense of basic trust never really develops, Erikson's theory would predict that it may be hard to acquire a strong sense of ego integrity.

In Erikson's (1950/1993) theory, stage number five often is considered the most important. It starts when puberty begins and from thereon covers the rest of adolescence (so up to age 18-ish) and covers the developmental task that this book is all about: acquiring a sense of identity as opposed to role confusion. Erikson (1950/1993, pp. 261–262) described identity as ". . . the accrued confidence that the inner sameness and continuity prepared in the past are matched by the sameness and continuity of one's meaning for others". If you read Chapter 1 and Chapter 3, I hope you remember this means that identity is about feeling like the person that you are now is much like the person you were before and anticipate to be in the future. It is also about making sense of having different roles in different situations, but that all those roles are part of who you are and are somewhat logically related to each other. Lastly, a sense of identity should help you to see yourself as unique relative to others. This uniqueness is not about being better or worse, but just different and distinguishable from others in your environment.

Developing a sense of identity becomes important in adolescence because in most cultures there is a role change around then. Youth are expected to no longer simply rely on the teachings of caregivers and others but to become adults who are more responsible for themselves. Erikson (1950/1993) pointed to the importance of adjusting and rethinking childhood teachings to fit with your own inner desires and the opportunities offered in the social roles that are available in the society you are part of at a given moment in time. In that sense, it is identity development that allows youth to adapt to a changing society and, for example, consider careers that weren't available to their parents, such as influencer or professional gamer. Before I create a moral panic with pointing to these careers, I will say that (a) Erikson had never heard of those two professions (he passed away in 1994) and (b) that his writings do suggest that it is important to be realistic in career choices. Also consider this: for a few weeks in some summer in the 1990s I took over my cousin's local newspaper delivery job, which is a job that in many places is no longer available. It is also far from the only job that has become less widely available or disappeared altogether! In other words, society changes and the process of identity development allows us to adapt to those changes.

Erikson (1950/1993, 1968/1994) also described phenomena that may occur when people temporarily feel lost in the process of figuring out who they are. This includes a strong orientation to same-aged peers, so wanting to spend a lot of time with your same-aged friends or classmates and putting a lot of value in their opinions about you. Somewhat related to that is a tendency towards in-group ("us") versus out-group ("them") thinking. Then there is a strong attraction to idols, or sometimes more specifically exemplars. Put more simply, in search of identity we may pick people who we want to be like and then try to become like them (Klimstra et al., 2023). This attraction to "idols" along with the confusion that can arise when figuring out who you are, can also lead to a temporary attraction to ideologies that seem to provide answers to all of life's complex questions: extreme ideologies (Erikson, 1950/1993). As you read this list, you may think that all of the above can also apply to adults of any age. Erikson would have agreed with you. You don't even have to open a book for the evidence of that, as one of his books went by the title *Identity and the Life Cycle* (Erikson, 1980).

Overall, Erikson generated a lot of interest in identity with *Childhood and Society*. It was a best seller and won prestigious book awards. However, for specific ideas on identity development, *Identity: Youth and Crisis* is the go-to (Erikson, 1968/1994). Despite all the strengths of Erikson's work, many researchers felt that there was a need to further elaborate on his rather broad ideas. This mostly led to "mid-range" theories which will be covered in Chapter 6. However, one broad theory that is perhaps only a tiny bit narrower in attempting to explain personality development across the life course is McAdams's theory.

McAdams's theory of personality development

Reading this subheading you might feel cheated because the topic suddenly changed to personality development. If that really is how you feel, hold on! The only reason to cover a theory on personality development here is because narrative identity (also described in Chapter 3) plays a key part in it. But let's first clarify the distinction between personality and identity. In everyday life those are sometimes used interchangeably, making the difference between the two unclear to many people. You should by now know what identity is about, so let's focus on personality. **Personality** was originally defined as "the dynamic organization within the individual of those psychophysical systems that determine his unique adjustments to his environment" (Allport, 1937, p. 48)[1]. That is a rather broad

> **Personality** Using an adapted version of Allport's original definition, it is a wide set of factors that describe a person and their adjustment to the environment, and this set of factors, as well as the factors themselves can (and do) change across time.

definition, similar to how personality is defined in the theory by McAdams (2015) that is covered in this section. According to such definitions, someone's identity can be considered part of their personality, but someone's personality would not be considered part of their identity.

McAdams (2015) proposed **three lines of personality development** that mutually influence each other. The specific combinations of these three lines can help you understand what a person is like. It is a developmental theory as it attempts to explain stability and change in personality across the life course and proposes that the different lines of personality change in relevance at different ages. These three lines of personality are about the person as (1) a social actor, (2) a motivated agent, and (3) an autobiographical author.

Three lines of personality development McAdams's theory which suggests that we start out in life as social actors, later in childhood also become motivated agents with our own goals, and in adolescence and young adulthood also become an autobiographical author. The "also" is important here, as even adults are still social actors in addition to being motivated agents and autobiographical authors.

Infants already show individual differences in temperament, like for example their tendency towards smiling and being excited. These tendencies are often considered part of a broader temperamental dimension called positive affectivity. Later in life this would be called a personality "trait"[2] dimension. Most likely, it'd be referred to as extraversion which is one's tendency to be outgoing and assertive. It is called a **dimension** because it's not something that you either have or do not have, but something that some have more of than others. In other words, it's like the outside temperature: there's never "no" temperature, it's always somewhere on a continuum from very hot to very cold. The kind of dimensions used to describe temperament are broad as they summarize a whole lot of comparable tendencies. This might be a little imprecise, but it makes communicating

Dimension A characteristic, or variable, that is not something that you either have or do not have, but something that some have more of than others, or that you yourself have more of at some points compared to another point in time.

about people easier. Just think about describing someone in, for example, 500 specific characteristics. That's a whole lot more complicated than summarizing all of that in just three-or-so broader characteristics.

Specific to temperament, there is of course more than just positive affectivity (see Shiner et al., 2012, for an overview of temperament and its dimensions), but the idea is that people can be described along a limited number of dimensions that describe relatively stable tendencies. These broad "trait" dimensions form the first line of personality development, with the person as a social actor. That means that you could say they act out these "traits" with other people reacting to those. Just think about it: you probably react differently to someone who is very extraverted compared to someone who is more reserved.

When children reach age 6–7, their personalities are thought to become more complex. They are no longer only social actors, but also become motivated agents (McAdams, 2015). In other words, they start forming longer-term goals and become capable of planning. Also, their thoughts, behavior, and emotions are no longer just based on their "traits", but also partly driven by their motives. That is, after age 6–7 children may no longer just behave in an outgoing way because they typically are extraverted, it could also be that they are trying to become friends with a classmate and think that they will be more likely to succeed with that if they act in a more outgoing way than is typical for them. You could say that their personality gets another layer as goals and motives are added onto the "traits" layer.

Then, typically somewhere in adolescence or young adulthood, so roughly between ages 12 and 25, people start to form their own personal life stories (McAdams, 2015). They become authors of their own autobiography. As most of us won't ever write a book about ourselves, "autobiography" here just refers to the stories about ourselves that we carry with us in our memories and that we live by. Obviously, children tell stories, too, but their stories are about things like exciting bike races with other kids in the neighborhood, or a family visit in a far-away town (maybe just 30 minutes away, but that can feel like a lifetime for both children and their parents!). The kind of autobiographical life stories that tend to first show up between age 12 and 25 are different. They are about specific episodes that we think describe us for who we are and that give meaning to our life. As described in Chapter 3, these life stories represent our narrative identity. They form a third line of personality development, making the personality of the typical adult yet more complex than that of a typical 10-year-old.

The way this works is that if people form an autobiographical account about themselves as being outgoing, they might start acting more outgoing to confirm their autobiographical account. Similarly, if I see myself as great planner and I would have missed a bunch of deadlines for finishing this book, I wouldn't be so happy as it wouldn't fit my own autobiographical account. Depending on how important this book would be to my narrative identity, I might even change my life story, de-emphasizing my planning skills. That might then make me become less inclined to try planning other parts of my life. In other words, as autobiographical accounts change, eventually our "traits" or our goals and motives might change with them. However, typically our autobiographical stories are at least somewhat related to the "traits" and the goals and motives we had earlier in life.

An important thing to remember is that these three parts of our personality, so the person as actor, as motivated agent, and as autobiographical author, continuously influence and interact with each other. So, in McAdams's (2015) theory, people's narrative identities are the last part of their broader personality to fully develop, but it is an important part that can substantially affect the further development of the parts that were already there. In other words, when trying to answer the question "who are you" through a narrative perspective, the answer doesn't come out of nowhere. It usually is related to your earlier personality development and will likely affect your future personality development.

Dynamic systems theory

Dynamic systems theory (DST) can be applied to many different topics. When applied to the study of human development, the central focus is on the development of a particular individual. This contrasts with theories like the ones discussed earlier in this chapter, which often focus on more general patterns of development common across groups of people. To explain the development of a particular phenomenon, it is important to identify its key components and contributing factors. For identity development, commitment and exploration are thought to be important, but so is conflict (Kunnen, 2019). Conflict here is not about arguments with others,

> **Dynamic systems theory (DST)** A broad theory, which (when applied to identity) describes and explains identity development in terms of complex, ever changing interactions between an individual and all of the factors in their environment. This is not to say that identity development is chaos according to DST, as humans and their interactions with the environment can be described as self-organizing systems.

it's about a mismatch between what your current commitments look like and what is required, expected, or appreciated in the specific context you are in. For example, imagine it's the early 2000s and you are working on a project in engineering school that has the specific goal of developing DVDs (you might have to look up what those are/were . . .) that can store 10 times as much data compared to the standard at the time. You are truly becoming an expert on this and are already imagining the job offers you'll get from the big companies in the DVD market. However, then everybody starts using cloud services for data storage. Having a career in that would require a whole different skillset. That'd be a conflict between your commitment to having a career in DVD engineering and changes in the context, which in this case is "the market"! You could probably imagine how this could weaken your commitment to your project and engineering school more generally, and it might lead you to explore alternative careers. There are a whole lot of different ways to deal with such conflicts, which could include rethinking the situation and, when applied to the DVD-expert example, seeing the acquisition of new skills as a strength that one can widely apply to a variety of situations. That could certainly be interpreted as identity development and would be referred to as assimilation (for similar examples, see Kunnen, 2019). Another, more drastic, strategy would be to stop the DVD project and with that abandon your career plan. In other words, you'd replace your commitment with something else (maybe a career in bicycle engineering). That'd be referred to as accommodation.

The example above may suggest that identity conflicts are easy to detect. However, that's often not the case, partly because people may not be fully aware of them. They might feel like something is not quite right, but they don't know what. Emotions signal to us and those around us that something is going very well (in case of positive emotions) or not so well (in case of negative emotions). For that reason, emotions also have a prominent role in this theory and indeed have been shown to be strongly related to identity processes (van der Gaag et al., 2017).

Regardless of whether people are directly aware of identity conflicts, there are large individual differences in how they solve them. Those may be caused by a variety of factors, including but not limited to their success with strategies they previously used and the power they have to affect the environment they're in. In other words, one person's identity development may look very different from that of another person.

To further complicate things, there are also many reasons for specific individuals to deal with identity conflicts differently at different points in their life. Personally, I navigate my identity rather differently now that I'm in the United States compared to when I was in my home country. This is because my position in society has changed, for example in terms of what my rights are as a non-citizen green card holder in the United States compared to being a citizen in The Netherlands. Beyond this, things happen to us that we have no control over, like pandemics and economic recessions, which can affect our identity, too. All of this means that our identities don't just grow stronger over time, which is how Erikson's (1950/1993) theory sometimes has been interpreted (which is not to say that that's what he said!). DST accounts for this by describing identity development as characterized by continuous ups and downs in our commitment strength (Kunnen, 2019). Those ups and downs aren't random according to DST, they reflect that humans and their complex interactions with the environment can be described as self-organizing systems.

Broader socio-contextual factors and their influence on identity

The previously discussed theories already make some reference to the importance of the context for identity development. However, several other theoretical frameworks focus on this more directly and specifically. This section will discuss several of these theoretical perspectives.

One first such perspective is provided by the identity capital model briefly mentioned in Chapter 3. The model derives its name from the idea that societal change has created a situation in which people increasingly have to rely on a personal identity to navigate life. This makes a sense of identity an important resource or, in other words, "capital" (Côté, 2002). That identity capital can be fed by resources including factors such as self-esteem and sense of purpose in life, but also by factors such as membership of groups such as sororities or fraternities, one's educational record, and factors related to social class such as parental social status and financial resources. Individuals are all different in terms of these resources, and their resources may also be more useful in some contexts than others. Fo example, past affiliation with a particular sorority or fraternity may help for getting some jobs but could be frowned upon if you try to make a career in another field. As another example, some people easily develop a strong educational identity in high school in part because they are good at navigating relationships with their peers and teachers. Others who are less sociable may struggle with that but still easily develop a strong career identity, because their strengths (perhaps effectively working independently) happen to fit numerous career options that seem exciting to them.

The identity capital model points to the role that social class has in identity development but is less clear about the role of race. Probably the most prominent theory on the role of race in identity development is the **phenomenological variant of ecological systems theory** (PVEST; Spencer et al., 1997). There are five components that feature in PVEST (Spencer, 2021). First, there is the net vulnerability level which includes everything that can bring challenges to an individual's development in the context of **marginalization**. This could be race, gender, socio-economic status, and also temperamental factors. Second, the net stress engagement level is the extent to which such challenges actually are encountered. If that happens, the third component is required, reactive coping methods. These reflect how people engage with stressors in a particular moment. However, individuals may repeatedly encounter stressors and as a result they may develop relatively stable ways of coping with those stressors. Those stable coping responses are referred to as emergent identities and are the fourth component of PVEST. These emergent identities, in turn, are related to the fifth and final component: decision-making and problem-solving strategies referred to as life-stage-specific coping outcomes. All components are thought to influence each other, but the main emphasis is on how systemic factors, such as oppressive systems that favour some groups and marginalize other groups, can shape identity development.

Phenomenological variant of ecological systems theory (PVEST) A theory which describes and explains how systemic factors, such as oppressive systems that favour some groups and marginalize other groups, can shape identity development.

Marginalization A process through which members of some groups in society are placed in a position in which they have little power, much less than other groups.

The definition of identity in PVEST is closest to the coherence function of identity described in Chapter 1. However, identity also provides continuity, often operationalized through commitment and exploration processes (see Chapters 1 and 5). How those processes can be affected by racial stereotypes and racial biases has also been outlined (Park & Johnson, 2024). To give just one example, racial stereotypes and biases can stop, or at least discourage, people from exploring certain identity options. In sum, being considered part of a **social category** based on one attribute such as race and the marginalization and privilege associated with this can already have a profound impact on identity development.

> **Social category** A group of people defined by a common attribute, such as a group defined by a particular racial category (e.g., Black people in the United Kingdom).

Things get even more complicated if multiple social categories, such as race and gender, are both involved. This is where **intersectionality** becomes relevant. Intersectionality was first described by Crenshaw (1991) to explain discrimination of Black women in the United States. However, it has been applied to other groups and other societies as well. Intersectionality refers to the idea that to understand the full complexity of discrimination, one needs to not just focus on discrimination based on race or gender and not even "add up" discrimination based on those two. It is about particular combinations of social groups. For example, systemic oppression based on gender can exist across all racial groups but still work differently in those different groups. Similarly, systemic oppression based on race can affect all gender groups, but depending on what gender group you are part of it creates different issues.

> **Intersectionality** The idea that the effects of being part of multiple marginalized groups do not simply add up. Instead, being part of one marginalized group will have different effects in terms of marginalization depending on what other groups (for example based on gender) you are part of.

The idea of intersectionality was not originally developed to explain the life of individuals, but to understand and highlight "systems of power, privilege, and oppression that are built into society's laws, policies, values, and practices" (Rogers & Syed, 2021; p. 604). However, individuals develop in context, so whatever happens in society affects the individual. Obviously, that doesn't mean that individuals who share the same combination of social categories (in this case Black women in the United States) are going to be similar in terms of their identity development as everyone's unique lived experiences are important, too.

To further clarify the links between intersectionality and identity development, Rogers and Syed (2021) proposed to examine identity and intersectionality at the personal, relational, and structural level. In other words, they first explained how children and adolescents talked about the intersections of race and gender (but you could replace that with, for example, social class, ethnicity, and sexuality) affecting them personally, so how for example being a white boy mattered to their understanding of who they are, in other words, to their identity. The relational level may not seem very identity-like at first sight, but when you describe how you see yourself in relation to others you are still answering a "who am I?" question. In those answers, there again can be reference to intersectionality if you compare how you are treated by others compared to how you think you would have been treated had you been part of a group based on a different combination of race, ethnicity, gender, sexuality, social class, etc. Finally, there is the societal level, for which intersectionality was originally intended. When combined with identity, this refers to how references to systemic privilege and oppression are incorporated in self-views. At the personal, relational, and societal level, individuals tend to think differently about themselves at different ages considering systemic inequality related to combinations of social categories. As they grow older, they may be more aware of being confronted with oppression and marginalization, and they may have encountered more instances of discrimination. They may then incorporate these experiences into their identity, making intersectionality highly relevant for understanding identity development.

A final way in which the context can shape identity is through the master narratives that were extensively discussed in Chapter 2. There they were described as culturally shared stories, and they certainly are! However, not everyone plays an equal role in shaping master narratives. Those with authority and those who have earned or unearned power and privilege can spread stories to the masses (e.g., through mass media such as social media) and with that spread and sustain master narratives (McLean & Syed, 2016). In other words, power plays a role in what the master narratives are, and unfortunately power is rarely equally distributed in societies.

Obviously, you can't be forced to adopt a master narrative, but resisting one and constructing an alternative can put elements in your personal narrative identity that otherwise would not have had to go in there. A clear example highlighted by McLean and Syed (2016) is about sexuality. In most societies, the master narrative about sexuality involves an expectation that over the course of development people will become attracted to someone of the opposite sex. The English language is particularly clear about this norm by referring to heterosexuality with the word "straight". Because of this norm, people deviating from the social expectations that come with it are expected to "come out" (note that a similar case can be made for deviating from social expectations around gender). Over the course of history, there has often been legislation restricting gay individuals and couples from having the same opportunities as heterosexual individuals and couples. Legislation has changed in several countries over the last few decades, with people identifying as gay no longer being criminalized and getting marriage rights. Research conducted in the United States showed that, parallel to this, the personal narratives of gay individuals also changed, with there being more variation among, and personal expressiveness in, the personal narratives, or narrative identities, of those who were part of younger generations when compared to older generations (Hammack & Cohler, 2009).

Another example of how deviating from the master narrative can be challenging relates to social expectations for women (McLean & Syed, 2016). Historically in many countries, the master narrative has been that for women, when compared to men, having children and taking care of children is more important. Still, resistance has created alternative narratives that emphasize the importance of women retaining financial independence and thus a career. Given the strength of both the master narrative and the alternative, research has shown that for women it can be a balancing act to negotiate expectations around having more of a caregiver role and having a successful career. Although gender inequality has decreased over the last 100 years in many places around the world, such negotiation processes are still less expected from men. This makes it less likely for men compared to women to have caregiving-career conflict become a part of their personal narratives, and thus their narrative identity. So, there may be fewer constraints on how men answer the "who am I" question.

Conclusion

You now are familiar with there being different types of theories in terms of scope. In this chapter we covered very broad ones, so theories that can explain an extensive and more general perspective on the "how" and "what" of identity development. In the next chapter, somewhat more specific theories will be covered: ones that can explain broad aspects, but not the full picture. These will be referred to as mid-range theories on identity development.

Notes

1 Unlike what Allport's definition may suggest, personality researchers at least nowadays think that those with pronouns other than he/him/his also have a personality.
2 I usually write "traits" with quotation marks because this word could suggest that they are largely genetically determined and unchangeable, which they are not (e.g., Lerner & Overton, 2017)! Views that people are the way they are and can't change have been proven

untrue, and worse than that: they have wreaked a lot of havoc over the course of human history. So, when I use quotation marks for "traits" I do so to make it clear that I do not endorse biological determinism and only use the word because it's widely used to describe personality and temperament dimensions such as positive affectivity and the Big Five of personality (i.e., conscientiousness, agreeableness, neuroticism, openness, and extraversion).

Further sources

1. Gaines Jr, S. (2019). *Personality psychology: The basics.* Routledge.

   If you'd like to know more about personality as discussed in this chapter, check out this book (or another introduction to personality psychology). As someone who has also taught personality psychology classes, I encourage you to do so as personality is almost as interesting as identity!

2. International Society of Research on Identity webinar with Prof. Dan McAdams; https://www.youtube.com/watch?v=Tsjzy4AAtog

   A great way of getting to know about why someone came up with a theory, is to hear them talk about it themselves! Here's a recording of a webinar in which McAdams discusses his ideas and his life, mixed with humor.

References

Allport, G. W. (1937). *Personality: A psychological interpretation.* Holt, Rinehart, & Winston.

Côté, J. E. (2002). The role of identity capital in the transition to adulthood: The individualization thesis examined. *Journal of Youth Studies, 5*, 117–134. https://doi.org/10.1080/13676260220134403

Crenshaw, K. (1991). Mapping the Margins: Intersectionality, identity politics, and violence against women of color. *Stanford Law Review, 43*, 1241–1299. https://doi.org/10.2307/1229039

Creswell, J. W., & Creswell, J. D. (2022). *Research design: Qualitative, quantitative, and mixed methods approaches* (6th ed.). SAGE.

Erikson, E. H. (1950/1993). *Childhood and society.* Norton.

Erikson, E. H. (1968/1994). *Identity: Youth and crisis.* Norton.

Erikson, E. H. (1980). *Identity and the life cycle.* Norton.

Hammack, P. L., & Cohler, B. J. (2009). Narrative engagement and stories of sexual identity: An interdisciplinary approach to the study of sexual lives. In: Hammack, P. L. & Cohler, B. J. (Eds.), *The story of sexual identity: Narrative perspectives on the gay and lesbian life course* (pp. 3–22). Oxford University Press. https://doi.org/10.1093/acprof:oso/9780195326789.003.0001

Klimstra, T. A., Archer, A., Chung, J. M., Reitz, A. K., & Engelen, B. (2023). There goes my hero: The role of exemplars in identity formation. *Human Development, 67,* 154–169. https://doi.org/10.1159/000531435

Kunnen, E. S. (2019). Identity development from a dynamic systems perspective. In: Kunnen, E. S., Ruiter, N. M. P., Jeronimus, B. F., & Gaag, M. A. E. (Eds.), *Psychosocial Development in Adolescence* (pp. 146–159). Routledge.

Lerner, R. M. (2018). *Concepts and theories of human development* (4th ed.). Lawrence Erlbaum.

Lerner, R. M., & Overton, W. F. (2017). Reduction to absurdity: Why epigenetics invalidates all models involving genetic reduction. *Human Development, 60,* 107–123. https://doi.org/10.1159/000477995

McAdams, D. P. (2015). Three lines of personality development: A conceptual itinerary. *European Psychologist, 20,* 252–264. https://doi.org/10.1027/1016-9040/a000236

McLean, K. C., & Syed, M. (2016). Personal, master, and alternative narratives: An integrative framework for understanding identity development in context. *Human Development, 58,* 318–349. https://doi.org/10.1159/000445817

Park, Y., & Johnson, S. K. (2024). A theoretical framework of the role of racism in adolescent personal identity development: Applications to racially marginalized youth in the USA. *Human Development, 68,* 44–60. https://doi.org/10.1159/000536141

Rogers, L. O., & Syed, M. (2021). Conceptualizing the multiple levels of identity and intersectionality. In: Bamberg, M., Demuth, C., & Watzlawik, M. (Eds.), *Handbook of Identity* (pp. 604–626). Cambridge University Press.

Shiner, R. L., Buss, K. A., McClowry, S. G., Putnam, S. P., Saudino, K. J., & Zentner, M. (2012). What is temperament now? Assessing progress in temperament research on the twenty-fifth anniversary of Goldsmith et al. (1987). *Child Development Perspectives, 6,* 436–444. https://doi.org/10.1111/j.1750-8606.2012.00254.x

Spencer, M. B. (2021). Acknowledging bias and pursuing protections to support anti-racist developmental science: Critical contributions of phenomenological variant of ecological systems theory. *Journal of Adolescent Research, 36,* 569–583. https://doi.org/10.1177/07435584211045129

Spencer, M. B., Dupree, D., & Hartmann, T. (1997). A Phenomenological Variant of Ecological Systems Theory (PVEST): A self-organization perspective in context. *Development and Psychopathology, 9,* 817–833. https://doi.org/10.1017/S0954579497001454

van der Gaag, M. A. E., Albers, C. J., & Kunnen, E. S. (2017). Micro-level mechanisms of identity development: The role of emotional experiences in commitment development. *Developmental Psychology, 53,* 2205–2217. https://doi.org/10.1037/dev0000336

Chapter 5

Explaining broad aspects of identity development but not the full picture

Mid-level theories

The previous chapter covered relatively broad theories, starting with Erikson's (1950/1993) theory on lifespan development with its large emphasis on identity. Several of the other broad theories covered in the previous chapter were also inspired by Erikson's work. This again is true for several more specific, or mid-range, theories that will be covered in this chapter (see also Chapter 3 for the links between theories). After starting with Marcia's identity status approach which directly built on Erikson's work, this chapter will cover two types of approaches that further elaborated on Marcia's work: the identity styles approach, and dual-cycle models to identity development. The final section covers motivated identity construction theory, which is less related to Marcia's work and more embedded in broader theories used in the social sciences. It aims to explain why people want to construct and change their identities.

Marcia's identity status approach

Erikson's (1950/1993) contributions were rather broad and primarily theoretical, which made it hard to directly translate his ideas into something that could be used in research. James Marcia (1966) addressed this by introducing the identity status approach, which made it possible to assess identity. At the core of this approach are the identity dimensions of commitment and exploration. Commitment reflects whether individuals have made a choice in a particular life domain and engage in activities to implement this choice, whereas exploration refers to comparing different potential commitments before choosing one (see also Chapter 1). However, Marcia (1966) primarily used levels of commitment and exploration to classify individuals into identity statuses. Crucially, he also focused on when exploration (had) happened and on where commitments came from. Based on this, he distinguished the four statuses shown in Table 5.1.

DOI: 10.4324/9781003557593-7

Table 5.1 Marcia's identity statuses

Identity Status	*Description*
Diffusion	Weak commitments, little to no exploration
Foreclosure	Committed, but these commitments were not formed after exploration and are more like "childhood identifications"
Moratorium	Weak commitments, but currently strongly exploring
Achievement	Strong commitments that were formed after a period of exploration

The identity status approach has been very popular in research on identity development and is still used. Developmentally, it has been proposed that most people would be expected to move from foreclosure and diffusion through moratorium towards achievement (Waterman, 1982). Research indeed found that if people's identity status changes it most commonly is a change towards identity achievement, especially as people move towards early adulthood (e.g., Kroger et al., 2010). However, contrary to what it might seem like at first sight, neither this theory nor the research on identity statuses suggest that identity development is over after you reach the achievement status. Sometimes you feel like you've got it all figured out and are very dedicated and motivated to pursue a particular career, but then you suddenly start questioning whether the direction in life you are taking is the right one. This may weaken your commitment and could make you start exploring again. In other words, you can move back to a moratorium status after you were in the achievement status. In fact, people move back and forth between all identity statuses! It is just that the pattern with change towards identity achievement is the most common one when people change. Interestingly though, the most common pattern overall is that people stay in the same identity status they were already in.

Research also shows that, on average, individuals in an "achievement" or "foreclosure" status often report having higher levels of psychological well-being (e.g., self-esteem) than those in other statuses (Ryeng et al., 2013). However, that doesn't mean that those other statuses, diffusion and moratorium, should be avoided. Going through a moratorium is necessary for reaching the achievement status, even though it is stressful for the time being. In addition, while a foreclosed identity status may be associated with high levels of personal well-being, it is also associated with being attracted to authoritarianism, which involves anti-democratic values and uncritical attitudes towards questionable authority figures such as dictators. This made Marcia (2013) comment that to avoid having ". . . a generation of authoritarian youth, we would be advised to provide sufficient educational resources, thinking exercises, and viable career opportunities to encourage identity construction rather than identity foreclosure, recognizing that the price might be an increase in stressful moratorium periods" (pp. 284–285). However, under other circumstances, for example when there is a strong expectation to follow in the footsteps of your parents and take over their business while few alternatives are available, foreclosure can be adaptive. Similarly, a diffused identity is not necessarily maladaptive: in an unpredictable and unstable environment it can be helpful to not explore much and to avoid strong commitments to remain flexible.

Also, unforeseen circumstances may force you out of a particular identity status. For example, in 2019 I signed a contract at my current employer in the United States to start working there in September 2020. I still had a contract at a university in The Netherlands at the time, told them that I would resign, and did so in early 2020. By then, there was some mention in the news of a virus going around in far-away places, but few people thought this virus would be responsible for the COVID-19 pandemic. At the height of COVID-19 no embassies or consulates were open so I couldn't get the required visa to go work in the United States while I had already resigned from my old job. In other words, I was forced out of a commitment by external circumstances and had to either hope that the embassies would open quickly (which they fortunately did about 3 weeks before my new contract started) or start exploring alternative options. In those uncertain weeks, options such as package delivery, working at one of the local grocery pickup points that had opened, and (more realistically) research consulting went through my mind. Due to my pretty-okay financial situation, I wasn't too stressed and because of what I knew about identity development I started reflecting on how interesting it was to be in a moratorium status. It also helped to have a colleague and friend who was in a similar situation (he had planned to, and eventually did, move to the United Kingdom).

In short, whatever the identity status is that you are in, you shouldn't label it as "good" or "bad", even if some statuses are on average associated with higher levels of well-being. Your status may work for you, because of your lived experiences and environment you're in, or may just be a logical consequence of the circumstances you find yourself in. The main thing to remember is that identity statuses are useful tools for describing where one is in their identity development, but being further towards achievement is not necessarily "better".

Marcia's identity status approach has been popular for many years and still is. However, it also has shortcomings that were increasingly recognized from the 1980s onwards. For example, an identity status is indeed a useful snapshot (or a "picture") of where individuals are in their identity development, but it is not very informative on how they got to that point (Bosma, 1985). Also, both commitment and exploration have been considered too broad to make sense of as there are multiple ways to explore and different ways to be committed (e.g., Bosma, 1985; Grotevant, 1987). Therefore, more refined models were needed. One set of such models are the so-called **dual-cycle models**, which will be discussed in the next section.

Dual-cycle models (of identity development) Theoretical models that describe identity development as occurring along two cycles: an identity formation cycle in which people construct commitments, and an evaluation/maintenance cycle in which people assess their commitments for whether they fit what they want. An assumption of these models is that people continuously move back and forth between the two cycles.

Dual-cycle models of identity formation and evaluation

To better capture ongoing exploration, the fact that there are different ways to explore, and (to a lesser degree) that there are different ways to commit, new models of identity formation were needed. Ultimately this led to two models of identity development, both of which had more dimensions than the two that Marcia (1966) had proposed. The first model distinguishes three dimensions and was proposed by Wim Meeus and Elisabetta Crocetti when they analysed identity formation among adolescents in The Netherlands (Crocetti et al., 2008). The first dimension, commitment, is described as reflecting the confidence that is derived from identity choices, so slightly different from how Marcia had described it. Specifically, according to this definition you'd be considered committed when you feel like something like your current major provides you with some certainty in life. Second, in-depth exploration describes reflection on current commitments without necessarily looking for alternatives. So, when you are thinking about what you could do in the future with your major in psychology without looking for alternative majors, you'd be engaged in in-depth exploration. If you would be having doubts about whether you want to continue with your current major and you're considering alternatives (maybe economics, history, or maybe quit university and get a full-time job), then you'd be involved in the third identity processes covered with this model: reconsideration.

Around the same time, Koen Luyckx (Luyckx et al., 2008) had proposed a similar model based on his work with college students in Belgium. He distinguished five identity dimensions. The first one, commitment making, is a lot like Marcia's commitment dimension as it reflects the extent to which a person is committed to follow a certain direction in life. The second, identification with commitment, is a lot like the commitment dimension of the three-dimension model (Crocetti et al., 2008) that was just discussed, as it's about the degree to which commitments provide certainty in life and whether people feel like those commitments match their values. Third, there is exploration in depth, which is pretty much the same as in-depth exploration. The fourth, exploration in breadth, has some similarities to the reconsideration dimension of the three-dimension model as it's about searching for something to commit to, but for exploration in breadth this search doesn't necessarily involve comparing alternative commitments to existing ones. In other words, if you are in your last year of high school and you are comparing a bunch of different options for what you're going to do after that, you'd be doing exploration in breadth, but not necessarily reconsideration. Finally, there is ruminative exploration, which was added because sometimes people get stuck when they are comparing a whole bunch of possible commitments. Many, if not all, of us have been there: you want to decide on a direction in life but instead of picking something, you keep yourself awake at night or your mind wanders off during the day because you are endlessly mulling over what direction to pursue.

The fact that these models are named dual-cycle models might at this point sound odd, as "dual" implies two and I just explained that the models have three and five dimensions. However, for both models those dimensions are part of two broader cycles: an identity formation cycle and an identity evaluation or maintenance cycle (Klimstra & van Doeselaar, 2017). When people are actively constructing or reconstructing their identity, they are in the formation cycle. They might seek to change specific commitments or to see what the most suitable option is by exploration in breadth and/or reconsideration. In other words, you'd be in the formation cycle when you're, for example, picking a major or considering changing your current major. Once you have new or "renovated" commitments in place, you may shift to an evaluation or maintenance cycle in which you are just figuring out what your commitments are like and/or what they may provide you with. In other words, you'd be doing exploration in depth. If you're in the maintenance/evaluation cycle and find out that your commitments won't get you to where you want to be, or if you find out that your commitments don't fit with your values, you might shift back to the formation cycle and look for different commitments.

In sum, dual-cycle models describe identity development as a continuous process in which you may move back and forth between formation and maintenance/evaluation of commitments. Because new challenges and opportunities keep on coming up, you may be in either cycle at any point in life. Take for example retirement or becoming a (great) grandparent: that may require both formation of new commitments and (re-)evaluation of old ones. At any point in this process, you may be mulling over your choices or lack thereof, so ruminative exploration may happen regardless of which cycle you are in at a particular moment in time. On the bright side: research does suggest that ruminative exploration tends to decrease with age (Weller et al., 2026). Aging isn't all bad!

The identity styles approach: Processing identity-relevant information

Marcia's model and dual-cycle models of identity formation are all about *what* people are doing identity formation-wise, or where they are in the development process. However, people are different in how they typically do this. To better account for individual differences in the *how* of identity development, the **identity styles** approach was developed in the 1980s by Michael Berzonsky. Berzonsky (2011) distinguishes three broad identity styles: an information-oriented style, a diffuse-avoidant style, and a normative style.

> **Identity styles** These are three different approaches that people use in addressing identity-relevant issues. The information-oriented style describes people who typically actively seek out, handle, and evaluate identity-relevant information. The diffuse-avoidant style describes people who seek to avoid or postpone dealing with identity-relevant information, or just let situations be leading in what they're doing. The normative style describes people who tend to adopt views from others (for example parents and other authority figures) when it comes to identity-relevant choices without much critical reflection on those choices.

To explain the differences between these styles, imagine wanting to reconsider your religious and spiritual orientation. What you could do is learn about a variety of world religions and the values associated with those and give yourself some time to think about the implications that each of these options would have for you. If that is how you typically handle such issues, then you'd have an information-oriented style. So, people who use an information-oriented style typically actively seek out, handle, and evaluate identity-relevant information. People who prefer this style tend to be in Marcia's (1966) identity achievement or moratorium status (Berzonsky, 2011).

Because religious and spiritual questions can be rather complicated and can have quite far-reaching implications, some people choose to avoid having to deal with such questions, postpone dealing with it, or just let situations be leading in what they're doing. If that's what someone is doing, and if this style of dealing with identity-relevant questions generalizes to other life domains such as career choice, they'd most likely have a diffuse-avoidant style. Given its name, it is probably not too surprising that people in Marcia's (1966) diffusion status often use this style (Berzonsky, 2011). This style might look like doing nothing, but that's not true. Take for example career decisions at the end of high school. Someone might let application deadlines pass because they can't decide on whether they'd like to go to college. As a result, they don't go to college but may take the first job that happens to come along. They'd then still have to adjust to the demands of that job, even though it would mostly be the situation that would dictate their adaptation process.

Religious and spiritual orientations also often run in the family. This could be because people adopt their parents' orientation after exploring alternatives and/or deep reflection on what their religion means to them. Alternatively, it could be because they adopted the views of their parents, or perhaps of friends, teachers, or others they look up to, without much critical reflection. Those who typically adopt views from others when it comes to identity-relevant choices without much critical reflection and evaluation of those choices, use what is referred to as a normative identity style. It probably sounds like Marcia's (1966) foreclosure status, and people with a foreclosed identity status are indeed likely to use this style (Berzonsky, 2011).

It can be tempting to think that an information-oriented style is the best and view other styles as less good, but that'd be a mistake. Berzonsky's (2011) work on identity styles is grounded in theories such as personal construct theory (Kelly, 1955), which can explain why it is wrong to consider some styles "better" than others. An assumption of personal construct theory (and therefore indirectly also Berzonsky's social-cognitive theory on identity styles) is that we are all born as "scientists" who try to make sense of the world around us. For that, we form ideas on how the world works and when those ideas are confirmed we keep them. When they don't work, we eventually replace them with others. To deal with the complexities of life, we apply our ideas to a wide set of situations, eventually turning them into broad patterns of thinking and with that also into broader problem solution styles. Identity styles are such styles.

In other words, people's identity styles are at least partly based on their lived experience, and thus on what worked well in the context they lived in. If a context is unpredictable, for example in a society with a rapidly changing job market or economic system, if the person in question doesn't really have all that much to choose from due to oppression or marginalization, or if there otherwise isn't time or (mental) energy available for extensive information-gathering and evaluation, styles other than an information-oriented one can be more adaptive (e.g., Vosylis et al., 2020).

The identity styles approach has been widely used and provides an interesting way of linking cognitive theories including the work of Jean Piaget (you may know this from a child development class) to identity theories that were grounded in psychoanalytic approaches. Key to remember is that the styles describe individual differences in people's go-to strategy for dealing with identity-relevant questions. In that, they are like personality characteristics and therefore relatively stable across time. However, relatively stable is not the same as perfectly stable! Identity styles do not just simply predict how people navigate their lives always and forever; they can also change as people navigate their lives. The same is true for what is covered in the next section: identity motives.

Motivated identity construction theory

The theories covered up to this point address how people develop an identity, but given how hard it can be to obtain a sense of identity you might ask why we'd go through all of that to begin with. **Motivated identity construction theory** (MICT; Vignoles, 2011) provides answers to this question. MICT brings together a series of motives that had been suggested across different literatures, literatures on both personal identity (which focuses on the "who am I" question) and social identity (which focuses on the "who are we" question; Vignoles, 2011). Many theories on social identity suggest that people primarily construct identities to gain positive self-views. This is referred to as the self-esteem motive. Another reason that is

> **Motivated identity construction theory** A theory that describes motives that people have for developing an identity. The theory emphasizes that there are both culture-specific and universal motives that can be applied to a variety of identities, that people usually have more than one motive, and that we're often not fully aware of our motives for constructing an identity.

frequently mentioned, both in research on social and personal identity, is that people have a need to see themselves as distinguishable from other people. This is referred to as the distinctiveness motive. The function of identity to provide us with a sense of distinctiveness was also mentioned in previous chapters.

In MICT, Vignoles (2011) recognizes many more motives for wanting to have an identity in addition to the ones that were just discussed. At least another four of those are thought to be universal. These are the continuity, meaning, efficacy, and belonging motives. Much like distinctiveness, continuity was also mentioned in previous chapters as a main function of what identity can provide us with. MICT emphasizes that people actively want an identity to attain a sense of continuity across time, as for many there is comfort in knowing that who you'll be tomorrow, or even a year or longer from now, is related to who you are right now, even in times when lots of other things change in your life.

The meaning motive reflects that some people may search for an identity to make their life feel (more) meaningful. If I had just been writing this book because I felt like it was something that needed to be done but that it could have been done by just anyone, it might have started feeling pointless. However, over the years I have developed an identity as a professor who likes to teach (especially in the field of identity and personality), and that makes my job in general, and the writing of this book specifically, feel more important to me in defining who I am.

When people have an efficacy motive, they search for an identity to feel more competent and more able to affect their environment. So, I might have also started writing this book and started building an identity as a textbook author to feel good about myself and feel more in charge of what I do with my life. Similarly, you may identify as a psychology student because it provides you with a sense of competence.

Finally, the belonging motive refers to the notion that feeling part of something bigger can be a reason to construct a particular identity. If I just went about teaching and didn't feel like I was a professor, I might feel a little lost on campus. It may be because I wanted to belong that I gradually started identifying as a professor over the years. Similarly, you might have started to describe yourself as a college student because you wanted to fulfill your need to belong.

Of course, MICT is about more than just a collection of motives for developing an identity. First, there is an important emphasis on culture. The six motives (self-esteem, distinctiveness, continuity, meaning, efficacy, and belonging) that were just described may be universal, but people from different cultures may pursue something like the meaning motive in very different ways. Perhaps the simplest way to clarify this is to think is about how people with different religious affiliations fulfill their meaning motive, through engaging in different practices.

Second, MICT stresses that people often aren't aware of their identity motives. We typically don't start seeing ourselves as, for example, a professor or student because we had an item on our calendar that said that we needed to work on our belongingness, feelings of efficacy, or sense of continuity. Still, such motives likely implicitly contributed to us developing such identities. So, the motives were there, we just didn't really think of those being the reason why we were developing a particular identity.

Third, in their quest to develop a sense of identity people are rarely guided by a single motive, but usually by multiple motives. Also, different people might develop the same kind of identity, but the motives that guide them to do so may be very different. Take for example an identity as a cyclist. When riding your bike around you might regularly be yelled and honked at by people in cars. To feel better about yourself, you might tell yourself that you put up with this because being a cyclist is important to you, and it makes you feel good about yourself. Then you'd have a self-esteem motive. It could also be that you came from a bicycle-friendly country with most inhabitants owning at least one bike, you moved to another country and have trouble making sense of that move but want to keep at least part of who you were before you moved. Would that be the case, you'd have more of a continuity motive. Perhaps you feel like you're just like everyone else in so many ways and you see a cyclist identity as a way of making yourself more distinguishable from others. In that case, you'd have a distinctiveness motive. As a reader, you are probably well able to come up with examples of adopting a cyclist identity because of meaning, belongingness, and efficacy motives, so it's easy to see how different motives can lead to adopting the same kind of identity.

Fourth and finally, identity motives can apply to different identities (e.g., gender, ethnic, national, career identity) and different identity processes (commitment, exploration, identity style, etc.). For example, motives can be used to understand why very different individuals commit to the same kind of career identity. In sum, MICT can help to make more sense of the "why" of identity change and stability across the course of the life span.

Conclusion

This chapter covered four so-called mid-range theories that focus on a particular aspect of the process of identity development. The first three theories that were covered are all related to each other and Erikson's broader ideas on identity development. The final one, motivated identity construction theory, is also related to social identity theories and theories on motives and goals. The next chapter covers theories that are even more specific or "narrow" as they aim to explain how our identities are related to specific aspects of our functioning.

Further sources

1. International Society for Research on Identity webinar with Prof. James Marcia; https://www.youtube.com/watch?v=Z9kGthMlkTU

   This webinar allows you to know about more of the life and work of Prof. James Marcia, in his own words. This is a great way of getting to know how researchers come up with concepts that turn out to be very influential!

2. Schwartz, S. J., Luyckx, K., & Vignoles, V. L. (2011). *Handbook of Identity Theory and Research*. Springer.

   This book was also recommended in Chapter 1, but as it covers chapters specifically on several of the theories covered in this chapter, it's also highly relevant here. Specifically, Chapters 2, 3, 4, and 18 of the Schwartz, Luyckx, and Vignoles handbook cover the theories in this chapter in a detailed manner.

References

Berzonsky, M. D. (2011). A Social-Cognitive Perspective on Identity Construction. In: Schwartz, S., Luyckx, K., & Vignoles, V. (Eds.), *Handbook of Identity Theory and Research*. Springer. https://doi.org/10.1007/978-1-4419-7988-9_3

Bosma, H. A. (1985). *Identity development in adolescents: Coping with commitments*. Unpublished doctoral dissertation, University of Groningen, The Netherlands.

Crocetti, E., Rubini, M., & Meeus, W. H. J. (2008). Capturing the dynamics of identity formation in various ethnic groups: Development and validation of a three-dimensional model. *Journal of Adolescence, 31*, 207–222. https://doi.org/10.1016/j.adolescence.2007.09.002

Erikson, E. H. (1950/1993). *Childhood and society*. Norton.

Grotevant, H. D. (1987). Toward a process model of identity formation. *Journal of Adolescent Research, 2*, 203–222. https://doi.org/10.1177/074355488723003

Kelly, G. A. (1955). *The psychology of personal constructs*. Norton.

Klimstra, T. A., & Van Doeselaar, L. (2017). Identity Formation in Adolescence and Young Adulthood. In: Specht, J. (Ed.), *Personality Development Across the Lifespan*, Elsevier. https://doi.org/10.1016/B978-0-12-804674-6.00018-1

Kroger, J., Martinussen, M., & Marcia, J. E. (2010). Identity status change during adolescence and young adulthood: A meta-analysis. *Journal of Adolescence, 33*, 683–698. https://doi.org/10.1016/j.adolescence.2009.11.002

Luyckx, K., Schwartz, S. J., Berzonsky, M. D., Soenens, B., Vansteenkiste, M., Smits, I., & Goossens, L. (2008). Capturing ruminative exploration: Extending the four-dimensional model of identity formation in late adolescence. *Journal of Research in Personality*, *42*, 58–82. https://doi.org/10.1016/j.jrp.2007.04.004

Marcia, J. E. (1966). Development and validation of ego-identity status. *Journal of Personality and Social Psychology*, *3*, 551–558. https://doi.org/10.1037/h0023281

Marcia, J. E. (2013). Afterword. *Identity*, *13*, 281–287. https://doi.org/10.1080/15283488.2013.799473

Ryeng, M. S., Kroger, J., & Martinussen, M. (2013). Identity Status and Self-Esteem: A Meta-Analysis. *Identity*, *13*, 201–213. https://doi.org/10.1080/15283488.2013.799431

Vignoles, V. L. (2011). Identity Motives. In: Schwartz, S., Luyckx, K., & Vignoles, V. (Eds.), *Handbook of Identity Theory and Research*. Springer. https://doi.org/10.1007/978-1-4419-7988-9_18

Vosylis, R., Erentaitė, R., & Klimstra, T. (2020). The Material Context of Adolescent Identity Formation: A Family Economic Stress Approach. *Identity*, *21*, 200–218. https://doi.org/10.1080/15283488.2020.1836491

Waterman, A. S. (1982). Identity development from adolescence to adulthood: An extension of theory and a review of research. *Developmental Psychology*, *18*, 341–358. https://doi.org/10.1037/0012-1649.18.3.341

Weller, J. A., de Moor, E. L., & Klimstra, T. A. (2026). Age patterns in dual-cycle identity processes and their associations with life satisfaction. *Journal of Personality*, *94*, 304–319. https://doi.org/10.1111/jopy.70001

Chapter 6

Theories on specific factors in identity development

Beyond the theories that represent broader ideas on how identity development unfolds, there is also theorizing looking into how more specific factors relate to identity development. Those more specific theories are the focus of this chapter. It is important to remember that "relate to" can mean different things. Some theories will contain ideas for what causes our identities to change. For example, could social media influencers cause our identities to change? Other theories could look at the consequences of identity development for specific aspects of our lives. They could for example aim to explain whether getting stronger commitments leads us to become happier. Yet other theories could address the fine and sometimes blurry lines between identity and other aspects of our lives. For example, one could say identity is related to happiness, but it's also possible to identify as a happy person.

The focus of this chapter will be on two topical areas that have been linked to identity development: social relationships, and the people we look up to (also known as exemplars). Keep in mind that the kind of topic-specific theories that will be covered in this chapter do not always focus on the larger context in which identity occurs. However, that doesn't mean that the researchers using these theories do not recognize that larger context.

Theorizing on identity and social relationships

The answer to the question "who am I" may sound like it's all about you, but other people in our environment have a substantial effect on how we see ourselves. This was already acknowledged in Erikson's (1950/1993) early work on identity development, but there are several more specific theories on this. One of these is identity control theory.

Identity control theory

Did you ever feel like the way others saw you in a particular situation didn't correspond with how you saw yourself? Did that motivate you to

DOI: 10.4324/9781003557593-8

change your behavior, your self-views, or maybe both? If so, you may have experienced what **identity control theory** (ICT) would predict. More formally, ICT (Burke, 2016) describes identities as control systems. It applies to role identities (e.g., what it means to be a student in a classroom), social identities (e.g., what it means to be part of a particular group, such as a specific ethnic group), and person identities (e.g., referring to personality characteristics, such as what it means to be tidy).

Identity control theory (ICT) A theory that describes identities as control systems, emphasizing that we may change a particular identity (e.g., your identity as a college student) if its meaning in a given situation repeatedly doesn't match our overall sense of what that identity means. So, if you generally think of yourself as a student who is always late on everything and you repeatedly see that you're among the first ones to turn things in, then you might start thinking of yourself as a student who is punctual.

ICT predicts that as we obtain an identity, we engage in behaviors that we think should go with the identity and then receive feedback from others on the appropriateness of those behaviors. Based on that, we develop a set of meanings, which are stored in what is referred to as the *identity standard*. However, in any given situation we also form an impression or *perception* of what it means to have this specific identity, typically from the feedback that others give us. This feedback could be things that are said to us, but also behavior of others towards us. According to ICT, we then use a *comparator* to assess whether our identity standard aligns with the perceptions of its meaning in that particular situation. If the *output* of the assessment of the comparator suggests a good enough match, then we keep the identity standard as is. If there is discrepancy, so if how we think we're perceived in a particular situation doesn't match our ideas of who we really are, then we can do two things. The easiest and most common thing to do is change our behavior so that we're perceived in a way that does match our identity standard. However, that's not always possible, for example because the way we think we are perceived by others is simply too different from who we think we really are (i.e., the mismatch between the identity standard and perception is too large). In such cases, we might then change our identity standard. In other words, there could be identity change as a result.

ICT is not necessarily a theory that is often used to explain identity development as defined in Chapter 1 as it focuses on very concrete and situational processes. However, developmental change does start somewhere, and we need to understand the in-the-moment processes that may set change in motion. Therefore, ICT is important for attempting to understand how specific factors may contribute to identity development.

Identity negotiation theory

Identity negotiation theory (INT; Swann & Bosson, 2008) also focuses on how identities are constructed, reshaped, and consolidated in interactions with other people. INT emphasizes that everyone who is involved in interactions brings in their own goals. The idea is that typically when we enter a situation, we consciously or less consciously have the goal to seek feedback from others that confirms our identity. For that reason, we present ourselves in a particular way. INT is very explicit about the fact that others bring their identity and goals into the interaction as well. However, explaining how identity change can work according to INT is easier when just focusing on one person, as in the example below.

> **Identity negotiation theory (INT)** A theory explaining how identities are constructed, consolidated, and reshaped in social interactions through feedback (e.g., by comments referring to what other people might think of us) and our reactions to that feedback.

Let's say you see yourself as very friendly person, and you enter a situation with other people present. What you will likely do is behave in ways that suggest to others that you are indeed a friendly person. Perhaps you'd even try a little harder when you're around people who don't know you yet, as you realize that they need a little more help to realize how friendly you really are. If you successfully convince others to see you as the friendly person you think you are, they will likely treat you in a way that suggests that they indeed think you're a friendly person. Conveniently, they may not even have to try that hard to make you think that they think you're friendly, because INT suggests that we tend to be biased towards information that confirms our identity. In other words, even if others behave somewhat ambiguously, you might decide that they decided you are indeed as friendly as you think you are.

All the above applies when your goal is to keep up the impression that you're friendly. However, being perceived as friendly is not always helpful, so sometimes even the friendliest people might consciously act out of character and behave angrily. INT suggests that taking on behaviors, or temporary identities, that are at first at odds with our longer-term, or "chronic", identities can lead to identity change. In our example, the person who started out as friendly and acted a little angry every now and then might be treated differently by others after a couple of minor acts of anger. Those slightly changed reactions of other people might then eventually lead the person to see themselves as less friendly compared to how they saw themselves before. And there you have it: a small identity change!

This was a brief overview of INT. For example, I only mentioned biased interpretation as a specific process affecting identity negotiation, whereas Swann and Bosson (2008) list several other relevant processes. They also explain how INT relates to other broader theories such as McAdams's work on personality and narrative identity (see Chapters 1, 3, and 4). There's only space here for providing you with the essential part of theories like this one and ICT, so if you want to know more, please consult the work that is cited in the respective sections.

Further theorizing on identity development and social relationships

In addition to more complete theories like ICT and INT, there are also smaller frameworks or ideas about identity development and social relationships. The first of those dates back to Erikson's (1950/1993) writings. As you might remember from earlier chapters, on the opposite pole of having a sense of identity there is role confusion. The idea is that when you start constructing your identity you likely experience at least some role confusion. To move past this, Erikson proposed that relationships could help, specifically through intimate conversations with others. Or, to quote him directly:

> To a considerable extent adolescent love is an attempt to arrive at a definition of one's identity by projecting one's diffused ego image on another and by seeing it thus reflect and gradually clarified. This is why so much of young love is conversation (Erikson, 1950/1993, p. 262).

Second, Erikson (1950/1993) pointed to the role of peer groups in protecting ourselves against a sense of role confusion. If people in a group are dressed alike, have similar interests, or share other characteristics, and then contrast those who "belong" to their group with those who don't, they may be doing this to protect themselves against identity confusion. In other words, young people may form cliques to become more distinct from some others (those outside of the clique), but not all others (they still need to feel like they are largely like those within their clique). The funny and sometimes seemingly illogical situations that can be caused by this have been nicely illustrated in popular media. Take for example a scene from the series *Derry Girls*, which centers around a group of teenagers growing up in the eventful 1990s in Northern Ireland. Before a new school year starts, they decide to be "individuals" by all wearing the same jeans jacket. However, on the first day only one of them, Clare, shows up with the jeans jacket, gets upset and says "Well, I'm not being an individual on my own!". This scene nicely illustrates how becoming an individual (gaining a sense of identity) is a gradual process in which most of us don't want to stand out from everyone right away.

Identity development is sometimes thought of as something that happens when you break free from your parents, but most identity researchers would argue that that's not necessarily the case. Two perspectives, by Grotevant and Cooper (1986) and Lichtwarck-Aschoff and colleagues (2008), specifically point to the importance of adolescents' relationships with caregivers. Both perspectives focus on two relationship characteristics: **autonomy** (or individuality) and **connectedness**. Autonomy is about acting out of your own initiative, whereas connectedness refers to responsiveness and sensitivity towards others and their views. Autonomy and connectedness may seem like opposing forces, but they are not. If you take a moment, you can probably think of an example in which you did something on your own initiative, but in doing so you still took the feelings, needs, and desires of others into account. Grotevant and Cooper (1986) argued that for adolescents to feel encouraged to explore their identity, they'd need to balance autonomy and connectedness. And indeed, the highest levels of identity exploration tend to be found among those who express both autonomy and connectedness in the relationship with their caregivers.

Autonomy The extent to which you feel like you are acting out of your own initiative, have control over what you do.

Connectedness The extent to which you are responsive and sensitive towards the needs and views of others.

Lichtwarck-Aschoff and colleagues (2008) also theorize on the links of autonomy and connectedness with identity development. They describe autonomy striving, so trying to get to a point where you feel like you're acting on your own initiative, as something that can set identity exploration in motion. Simply put, if you feel like you can act on your own initiative, you likely feel more ready to explore a variety of options for things like values and a general direction in life. Connectedness also needs to be reworked when adolescents start developing their own identity. The goal there is to move from a childlike version of connectedness with adolescents still feeling like they are largely dependent on their caregivers, to a form of connectedness that reflects a more balanced relationship. It takes time for such shifts to fully take shape, but identity development and changes in autonomy and connectedness can still be observed in real life in the form of conflicts and the emotions that come with these. In other words, conflicts aren't all bad! Do not see this as an invitation to fight your parents, friends, or partner on everything, but do know that conflicts can simply reflect a reconfiguration of relationships. In the longer run the results of such conflicts (if they're resolved in a decent way of course) can benefit everyone involved.

Important about the theoretical idea of Lichtwarck-Aschoff and colleagues (2008) is also that it emphasizes that our identities can change throughout the lifespan. Our current identity affects how we enter situations and behave in those; it is our "go-to" way of behaving in interactions with others. Eventually, what we encounter in those situations and how others react to us may contribute to changes in our identity. If that sounds a lot like the dynamic systems theory discussed in Chapter 4, that's no coincidence. That's the broad theory behind these ideas on the role of autonomy, connectedness, and conflicts in identity development.

Theorizing on identity development and exemplars

Somewhat related to the topic of social relationships is the idea that engagement with **exemplars**, so people we generally look up to, can be related to identity development (Klimstra et al., 2023). If these exemplars are our parents, friends, or someone living in our neighbourhood, then the ideas about the links between social relationships and identity development covered in the previous sections may apply. However, exemplars are often famous people, including those who are no longer among us. Regardless of who they are, exemplars can serve as inspiration for who we want to be like or even for clarifying our values to ourselves.

> **Exemplars** People who we generally look up to and therefore serve as models for the kind of person we want to become and the path we want to follow in life.

It's often easier to find out who you admire than to answer abstract questions like "what do you stand for", especially when you're a teenager.

So, let's say you admire U.S. singer Taylor Swift or U.K. football (or if you're American: soccer) player Marcus Rashford. That might be not just because you like her music or his ball handling, but because of their advocacy for social justice. When you read about their work on social justice, some of you may feel negative emotions such as disgust, or not much at all. However, if you feel what are referred to as **other-praising emotions** such as admiration, this might come with a realization that you stand for the same kind of social justice that they stand for. You can also see them as "possible selves" (see Chapter 3), so people who you literally might want to be like. In that case, you might want to make an attainable version of them because, unfortunately, we don't all have the talent of Taylor Swift or Marcus Rashford.

> **Other-praising emotions** Emotions such as admiration or elevation, which come up when we see others doing something we think is excellent.

Specific to Marcus Rashford, you might pick him as an exemplar because you play football, just like him. That's a far from unlikely possibility given the enormous numbers of people around the world who play football. In that case, you might primarily relate to him due to your shared passion for football and perhaps be inspired by his social justice advocacy as more of a side effect.

Those are just some ways in which we're inspired by (famous) others in our identity development. Do keep in mind that it's not all good to have an exemplar for identity formation. Especially if someone is presented to you (or forced upon you) by someone else as an exemplary person, you might look for everything you find annoying about them and not be motivated at all to become more like them! Nonetheless, finding out who you are or who you might want to become is sometimes easier when you have someone to look up to. Similarly, the character of someone who we look up to might already tell us a thing or two about who we are.

Conclusion

In this chapter, we covered a range of theories and theorizing about specific topics, primarily on social relations and exemplars. This book also contains theorizing at this level of specificity on the relationship between identity and mental health. Because that relationship is complicated but has direct implications for clinical practice as well as public health policy, Chapter 10 (part of the section on key impacts) is devoted entirely to this important topic.

Specific theories can be helpful, but in reality our identities aren't just affected by one specific thing such as one particular social relationship.

Instead, all the specific things that we covered in this chapter and many more things, plus all kinds of combinations between different factors, affect us all together at the same time. Therefore, keep in mind that as useful as the theories that we covered here are, it is important to also consider the "bigger picture" theories covered in Chapters 4 and 5 when you think about the how, what, and why of identity development.

Further sources

1. *Derry Girls* (https://www.imdb.com/title/tt7120662/)

   TV series about teenagers growing up in the tumultuous 1990s in Northern Ireland. You'll be able to see a lot of (dramatized) identity development in action. Try to link principles of the theories discussed in this chapter (I already did a little bit of that for you) and the previous two chapters to what you see when you watch the series.

2. Csikszentmihalyi, M. (2008). *Flow: The Psychology of Optimal Experience*. Harper Perennial.

   Classic book on optimal human functioning. Ideal way to get to know more about the roles of concepts like autonomy and connectedness.

References

Burke, P. J. (2016). Identity control theory. In: Ritzer, G., Rojek, C., & Ryan, M. (Eds.), *The Blackwell encyclopedia of sociology* (pp. 2202–2206). Blackwell Publishing. https://doi.org/10.1002/9781405165518.wbeosi002.pub2

Erikson, E. H. (1950/1993). *Childhood and society*. Norton.

Grotevant, H. D., & Cooper, C. R. (1986). Individuation in family relationships a perspective on individual differences in the development of identity and role-taking skill in adolescence. *Human Development, 29*, 82–100. https://doi.org/10.1159/000273025

Klimstra, T. A., Archer, A., Chung, J. M., Reitz, A. K., & Engelen, B. (2023). There goes my hero: The role of exemplars in identity formation. *Human Development, 67*, 154–169. https://doi.org/10.1159/000531435

Lichtwarck-Aschoff, A., van Geert, P., Bosma, H., & Kunnen, S. (2008). Time and identity: A framework for research and theory formation. *Developmental Review, 28*, 370–400. https://doi.org/10.1016/j.dr.2008.04.001

Swann, W. B., Jr, & Bosson, J. (2008). Identity negotiation: A theory of self and social interaction. In: John, O., Robins, R., & Pervin, L. (Eds.), *Handbook of personality psychology: Theory and research* (pp. 448–471). Guilford Press.

Section 3

Key methodologies

By the end of this section, you will:

- Be familiar with the most commonly used measures in the study of identity development.
- Know what quantitative and qualitative measures are and be able to name and explain several of each of these types of measures.
- Be able to explain validity and reliability, and evaluate specific identity measures for that.
- Be able to have taken questionnaires and tried out interviews and writing assignments used in the study of identity development.

DOI: 10.4324/9781003557593-9

Chapter 7

Measuring identity formation

Basic terminology and widely used measures

Up to this point, you have learned about the basic concepts of identity development and important theories on this topic. However, theories are only useful if they are eventually supported by evidence. To examine whether that's the case, identity needs to be measured. The measurement of identity and its development is the focus of the chapters in this section.

This chapter covers basic terminology used to describe approaches to measurement in the social sciences, including the study of identity. If you have already taken a research methods course, you could consider this section a refresher. Next, you will be introduced to some of the most widely used measures in identity development research: measures of identity formation. You won't just be able to read about those measures, you'll also be able to see them and try them out yourself.

Basics of measurement

> **Data** Simply put, it is information. Data are plural (singular would be datum), because to make sense of anything you always need more than one observation. In the context of the measurement of identity development, data are information that can be used to describe identity development for one person or a group of people.

Whenever you measure something, you will generate information which scientists refer to as **data**. Based on the type of data they generate, measures tend to be classified into broader categories. These broader categories are **quantitative measures** and **qualitative measures**. Quantitative measures generate data in the form of numbers. They can consist of questions in many forms, ranging from open-ended questions about someone's height or income to multiple-choice questions to rate someone's (typically your own) happiness, self-esteem, or

DOI: 10.4324/9781003557593-10

Quantitative measures Measures that produce data that comes in the form of numbers. Multiple-choice questionnaires in which you rate yourself on a scale (for example from 1 to 5) are an example of this.

Qualitative measures Measures that produce data in the form of anything other than numbers. An interview with open-ended questions would be one example, a task in which people would be asked to make a drawing (for example of their self-concept) would be another example.

Items The questions or statements that are part of a questionnaire.

perhaps commitment strength. As this book is about identity development, we'll stay with the commitment strength example, but know that you can exchange commitment strength for anything else in the paragraph below.

The type of quantitative measure that most people are familiar with are surveys on which you're asked to rate yourself on a bunch of characteristics. That could be in the form of questions (for example "how sure are you that your current direction in life works for you?"), statements (for example "the current direction I am pursuing in my life works for me"), or something related to those. Collectively, those questions, statements, and related things are referred to as **items**. Those items are then rated on a scale, for example from 1 to 5. The lowest number often stands for something like "not at all" or "very much unlike me", whereas the highest number tends to stand for something like "a lot" or "exactly like me". Usually there is more than one item for measuring a particular characteristic. Researchers then take the average or sum score across all of the items that examine that one characteristic (commitment strength) to know a person's score on that characteristic.

These and other kinds of quantitative measures lead to data that is expressed as numbers. Those numbers can be used to make comparisons. For example, you could compare everyone in your class to find out who has the highest level of commitment strength. You could also compare between groups, for example to see whether students from Leeds University in the United Kingdom on average have higher levels of commitment then those from Cambridge University in the United Kingdom. Yet another thing you could do is examine whether the commitment strength of a particular individual has changed between two time points (perhaps 5 years ago and now) or do something similar for a group of people. For example, you could measure students' commitment strength after they enroll in college, and right around the time they graduate, and then calculate the difference between those two averages. In sum, quantitative measures produce numbers which can be used for all kinds of comparisons. Whether those comparisons are always fair is a different story, so don't assume that what the numbers tell you is the absolute truth.

In contrast to quantitative measures, qualitative measures generate data that comes in the form of anything that's not numbers. This could be photos, videos, or really anything that isn't a number. Most commonly in the study of identity, qualitative data consists of language in the form of words. The kind of identity measures typically used to gather such data are interviews. Another very regularly used type of measure that generates qualitative data on identity are surveys with open-ended questions to which participants respond in the form of a couple of written sentences or something as long as a written story.

Both quantitative and qualitative measures are regularly used in research on identity. Whichever type of measure is used, it is important to examine its **reliability**, which indicates whether it produces consistent results. Examining reliability is not enough as a measure could consistently produce the same wrong results. You also need to examine **validity**, which indicates whether the measure examines what it is supposed to examine. There are multiple types of reliability and validity, extensively discussed elsewhere (e.g., Jordan & Hoeffer, 2011). This book covers regularly used identity measures and a general assessment of their validity and reliability, with some reference to subtypes of reliability and validity. The first measure to be discussed is one of the oldest: the identity status interview.

Reliability Whether a measure consistently measures the same thing. Just because a measure is reliable doesn't mean it's good as it could be consistently measuring the wrong thing! Therefore, reliability should always be assessed alongside validity.

Validity A measure is valid when it measures what it intends to measure.

The identity status interview

Most measures of identity development are in some way linked to James Marcia's (1966) **identity status interview**. The status approach and meaning of the statuses of diffusion, moratorium, foreclosure, and achievement was already covered in Chapter 5. Let's now look into how such statuses are measured with this interview.

The first thing that is important to know is that the identity status interview is a **semi-structured interview**. That means it is a type of interview that falls in between an **unstructured interview** and a **structured interview**. An unstructured interview is almost like an everyday conversation, so no specific questions are prepared. On the contrary, for a structured interview the interviewer has a full list of questions before they start and then they go through those during the interview. The semi-structured interview format of the identity status interview falls in between those, as the

Identity status interview One of the oldest identity measures. It is a semi-structured interview and based on people's responses they can be classified into four statuses: diffusion, foreclosure, moratorium, and achievement.

Semi-structured interview A type of interview that falls in between a structured and an unstructured interview. There is a guide with questions or topics, but interviewers can adapt the specific questions they ask depending on how the interview unfolds. Interviewers are also supposed to ask follow-up questions until they have sufficient information on the topic of interest.

Unstructured interview An interview that may almost look like a conversation. Typically, there are topics that the interviewer wants to address, but they come up with questions more or less "on the go".

Structured interview An interview in which all of the questions are predetermined. In other words, researchers know exactly what questions they'll ask beforehand.

interviewer has a guide with questions or topics, but they can adapt specific questions depending on how the interview unfolds.

With the identity status interview, Marcia (1966) assessed identity commitment and exploration in the two life domains of ideology (religious and political standing) and occupation. Based on that each person was classified into one identity status. The interviewer works from an interview guide with the broad questions and topics and then first asks questions to, for example, clarify what kind of job or career plans the interviewed person has. If the answer would be a career as a psychotherapist, then a next question would be "How willing do you think you'd be to give up going into *[a career as psychotherapist]* if something better came along?" (Marcia, 1966, p. 553). I inserted "a career as psychotherapist", but that's the part an interviewer would replace with whatever the person's career choice would be. You could also put a career in medical science, professional basketball, acting, or anything else there. Another example of a question is "Have you ever had any doubts about your religious beliefs?" (Marcia, 1966, p. 553) to test how firm the interviewees' religious commitments are. To see how this works in practice, James Marcia, who still occasionally publishes research, kindly agreed to interview an anonymous student. Check out the audio recording of this with the QR code below!

Based on the responses of participants, interviewers decide whether they obtained sufficient information for classifying their participants into an identity status. So, if the answer isn't very helpful, you'd ask more questions. That's not always an easy determination to make, so extensive training is required. This training focuses on the concepts of commitment and exploration as you can't know whether you have enough information if you don't know what you're looking for. Once all the information, or data, is in, researchers determine in what identity status someone fits. In other words, they engage in **coding** the interviews based on the obtained data. That means they categorize the large amount of data gathered with the interview into a smaller number of categories. Given that the interview can take 30 minutes or more (Marcia, 1966), you could probably imagine that there is a lot of data even from just one interview.

Coding The process of categorizing data before doing analyses.

Scoring manual A detailed document with guidelines for how to code data.

Interrater reliability If you perform observations or have conducted interviews, researchers often make sure that there is more than one person coding the responses. Those people are called raters. Interrater reliability reflects the agreement between two or more of those raters.

The coding of the interview data is a complex process in which researchers are guided by a **scoring manual**, which provides examples of what is characteristic of each of the identity statuses. Most researchers who apply the interview (including Marcia himself; see Kroger & Marcia, 2022) work with two coders, one of whom would ideally be the interviewer. With two coders, **interrater reliability** can be examined. This is relatively straightforward: if the two coders agree on the assignment of people to identity status, there would be high interrater reliability, whereas if they frequently disagree, interrater reliability would be low. As interrater reliability of the identity status interview tends to be high, it is considered a reliable measure of identity status. It has also been shown to be valid in a variety of ways. For example, the identity statuses tend to be associated with what you would expect them to be associated with based on theory, such as attachment and self-esteem (Kroger & Marcia, 2022).

In sum, the identity status interview has been crucial for the assessment of identity and its development. It's still used in 2025 and there's good reason for that: it provides very rich and detailed information. Still, there is the downside of it being time consuming to work with an interview, which limits how many people can feasibly be included in research with this measure. Therefore, several other measures have been developed. Of those, a series of multiple-choice questionnaires have become very popular.

Multiple-choice questionnaires on identity development

The first multiple-choice questionnaire that was developed to measure identity statuses and the underlying dimensions of commitment and exploration was the Objective Measure of Ego Identity Status. It was developed in the late 1970s, followed by later extended versions (Adams,

1998). Those measures, along with a couple developed by others, provided researchers with the possibility to study identity in situations where they or their participants didn't have a lot of time, and if they wanted to examine hundreds or perhaps even thousands of people in one study. Those questionnaires, along with critiques of Marcia's original theoretical ideas on identity statuses were at the basis of the questionnaires that have been popular since about 2010: the **Utrecht-Management of Identity Commitments Scale (U-MICS)** and the **Dimensions of Identity Development Scale (DIDS)**.

Utrecht-Management of Identity Commitments Scale (U-MICS) A measure with a multiple-choice format that is used to assess someone's scores on commitment, reconsideration, and in-depth exploration.

Dimensions of Identity Development Scale (DIDS) A measure with a multiple-choice format that is used to assess someone's scores on commitment making, identification with commitment, ruminative exploration, exploration in breadth, and exploration in depth.

The U-MICS and the DIDS both assess multiple identity dimensions to examine identity development from the dual-cycle perspective described in Chapter 5. Let's start with how the U-MICS works. Developed by Meeus and Crocetti (Crocetti et al., 2008) it is designed to measure the identity dimensions of commitment, exploration in depth, and reconsideration with 13 items in total. All items are statements to which you indicate your level of agreement on a scale from 1 (completely untrue) to 5 (completely true). If you follow the QR code link, you'll find the 13 items of the English-language version. It is also available in various other languages, so if your first language isn't English you might be able to find a version in your first language at https://www.elisabettacrocetti.com/u-mics/.

When you open the questionnaire, you'll see that the items are only about education. That is because the version presented there is the educational identity version of the U-MICS. There are versions for assessing identity in a wide variety of other life domains, such as career identity, parental identity, romantic identity, and many others. Making it suitable for another domain can be as simple as changing the word "education" to another word. You would then also need to retest the measure to see whether it is valid and reliable for the domain you're interested in, but the hard work isn't the rewording of the items. Try to think about a life domain you're interested in and see whether it would fit the item format!

Do consider filling out these identity items yourself as that can give you an idea of what it's like to participate in research on identity. If you fill the items out in a serious manner you can also calculate your average scores and interpret those using the instructions you'll find under the questionnaire if you follow the QR code link to the U-MICS.

Around the same time of the U-MICS, the DIDS was also developed. Luyckx and colleagues constructed it for use with college students (Luyckx et al., 2008). The DIDS is in many ways comparable to the U-MICS as it also uses multiple-choice items, also has a 5-point response scale (although the response options range from "strong disagree" to "strongly agree" instead of from "completely untrue" to "completely true"), it is available in various languages, and it has also been applied to multiple life domains. However, the vast majority of studies with this measure focus on one general "life domain": future plans. Another difference is the number of dimensions as there are five instead of three. These are commitment making, identification with commitment, exploration in breadth, exploration in depth, and ruminative exploration (see Chapter 5). More dimensions often means more items, so the DIDS comes with 25 of them. You can find all of those if you follow the QR code below. Much like with the U-MICS, you can calculate and interpret your own scores on the DIDS following the instruction there.

Much like the identity status interview, the U-MICS and DIDS have been extensively evaluated for their reliability and validity. They are considered very reliable. There's all kind of complicated calculations for that, but there are also more informal simple checks. For that, remember that DIDS items 1 to 5 are all supposed to measure commitment making. Therefore, you'd expect people to have a stable pattern of scores across those 5 items. In other words, if people have a score of 1 on item 1, they should also have a score close to 1 on item 2, 3, 4, or 5, and not score 5 on those. Of course, they could have slightly different scores on different items, as long as the general score pattern is pretty stable. People usually have such stable score patterns on commitment making and the other DIDS and U-MICS dimensions! So, people tend to respond in relatively consistent ways to items that are supposed to measure the same thing. That is what you would expect and indicates the measures are reliable.

Validity-wise, things also seem alright as the commitment and exploration levels are related to what you'd expect them to be related to, so things like parenting, self-reflection, and mental health (Crocetti et al., 2008; Luyckx et al., 2008). However, these multiple-choice questionnaires obviously don't measure identity and its development in a way that is as detailed as you could with the identity status interview. For example, it's hard to know where commitments come from with these questionnaires, whereas you can figure that out with the identity status interview (Kroger & Marcia, 2022). Therefore, these questionnaires are useful for examining identity and its development in large groups of people. They measure something related to what you measure with the identity status interview, just not the exact same thing.

The Identity Styles Inventory

In Chapter 5, identity styles were discussed as cognitive style preferences people have when dealing with identity issues. The Identity Styles Inventory was developed to assess these styles. Originally developed in 1989, the most recent version is the 5th edition (Berzonsky et al., 2013). Like the U-MICS and DIDS, it is a multiple-choice questionnaire that participants fill out by themselves. In other words, it is a **self-report measure**. The response scale runs from 1 ("not at all like me") to 5 ("very much like me") and the measure has subscales for each of the three identity styles: normative, informational, and diffuse-avoidant. All of those are measured with 9 items each, and a subscale to measure commitment as described by Marcia (1966) is also available. Here, the focus is on the identity styles items, of which you can find two examples for each of the scales in Table 7.1.

> **Self-report measure** A measure on which you report on something related to yourself. As identity is all about who you think you are, self-report measures are useful for this purpose.

Table 7.1 Example items for the Identity Styles Inventory – 5 (Berzonsky et al., 2013)

Normative Style	*Informational Style*	*Diffuse-Avoidant Style*
"I think it is better to adopt a firm set of beliefs than to be open-minded"	"Talking to others helps me explore my personal beliefs"	"Who I am changes from situation to situation"
"I strive to achieve the goals that my family and friends hold for me"	"I handle problems in my life by actively reflecting on them"	"I try not to think about or deal with problems as long as I can"

Note: The full list of items can be accessed with the QR code below.

As you can see, items for different styles nicely contrast with each other. That doesn't mean that you can't have a higher score on more than one style, as you could rely more on one style for one type of problem or decision and on another one under different circumstances. However, the idea is, and the research shows, that we do tend to have one preferred style. To translate this idea into "real" life, you could try and match characters from your favorite TV shows to each of the three identity styles.

Face validity Indicates whether a measure seems to assess what it is meant to assess. For example, if you know that identity development is about figuring out who you are, then for a measure to be face valid some of the questions should be relevant to figuring out who someone thinks they are.

Much like with the previously discussed measures, the Identity Styles Inventory has been thoroughly tested for its reliability and validity, and especially the most recent version does well in that respect. You can check for one type of validity yourself: **face validity**. Face validity is determined by checking whether the items seem to measure the theoretical construct (Jordan & Hoeffer, 2011). Therefore, you could go back to Chapter 5 and perhaps also consult the sources cited there. Once you have a good understanding of the identity styles, if you concluded that the questionnaire items indeed matched the styles, the measure would be face valid according to your assessment.

Conclusion

All the measures covered in this chapter were designed to assess constructs related to identity statuses. Most of the measures that were discussed are quantitative: multiple-choice surveys that come with numerical values or scores calculated for those who complete them. The original way to get to identity status measurement was an interview generating qualitative data, in this case information in the form of words, which was then used to classify individuals into groups. Of course, there are more aspects of identity that are important and measures for those have been developed as well. These kinds of measures will be covered in the next two chapters, starting with those designed for the measurement of narrative identity through life stories.

Further sources

1. Creswell, J. W., & Creswell, J. D. (2022). *Research design: Qualitative, quantitative, and mixed methods approaches* (6th ed.). Sage.

   If you want to know more about research methods in the social sciences, then this textbook is very helpful. It gives you an overview of everything involved in making decisions on research designs, including measurement.

2. Jordan, C., & Hoeffer, R. A. (2011). Reliability and validity in quantitative measurement. In: Thyer, B. A. (Ed.). *The Handbook of Social Work Research Methods* (pp. 52–67). Sage.

   This is a brief chapter that is helpful if you want to know more about reliability and validity. It uses relatively accessible language.

References

Adams, G. R. (1998). *The Objective Measure of Ego Identity Status: A Reference Manual.* [Unpublished Manuscript]. https://osf.io/fc52d/download

Berzonsky, M. D., Soenens, B., Luyckx, K., Smits, I., Papini, D. R., & Goossens, L. (2013). Development and validation of the revised Identity Style Inventory (ISI-5): Factor structure, reliability, and validity. *Psychological Assessment, 25*, 893–904. https://doi.org/10.1037/a0032642

Crocetti, E. (n.d.). *U-MICS.* Retrieved on June 2, 2025, from https://www.elisabettacrocetti.com/u-mics/

Crocetti, E., Rubini, M., & Meeus, W. (2008). Capturing the dynamics of identity formation in various ethnic groups: Development and validation of a three-dimensional model. *Journal of Adolescence, 31*, 207–222. https://doi.org/10.1016/j.adolescence.2007.09.002

Jordan, C., & Hoeffer, R. A. (2011). Reliability and validity in quantitative measurement. In: Thyer, B. A. (Ed.). *The Handbook of Social Work Research Methods* (pp. 52–67). Sage. https://dx.doi.org/10.4135/9781412986182

Kroger, J., & Marcia, J. E. (2022). Erikson, the identity statuses, and beyond. In: Bamberg, M., Demuth, C., & Watzlawik, M. (Eds.), *The Cambridge Handbook of Identity* (pp. 215–237). Cambridge University Press. https://doi.org/10.1017/9781108755146.012

Luyckx, K., Schwartz, S. J., Berzonsky, M. D., Soenens, B., Vansteenkiste, M., Smits, I., & Goossens, L. (2008). Capturing ruminative exploration: Extending the four-dimensional model of identity formation in late adolescence. *Journal of Research in Personality, 42*, 58–82. https://doi.org/10.1016/j.jrp.2007.04.004

Marcia, J. E. (1966). Development and validation of ego-identity status. *Journal of Personality and Social Psychology, 3*, 551–558. https://doi.org/10.1037/h0023281

Chapter 8

Measuring narrative identity

How to make sense of the stories of other people's lives

Of the measures you read about in the previous chapter, only the Identity Status Interview produces data in the form of something other than numbers, spoken language. The focus of this chapter will be on the analysis of life stories for the purpose of learning about someone's identity. Life stories tend to come in the form of spoken or written language. Chapter 3 and 4 covered that in the 1970s and 1980s social scientists started to appreciate life stories again after they had been pushed into the margins for decades. It was McAdams (1985) who argued that identity could be viewed as a life story. More specifically, narrative identity was defined as an evolving story, or set of stories, that we carry along (not literally, just metaphorically) and live by. The story has characters, plots, and scenes, which can be studied and analyzed.

In this chapter, you will learn about techniques that researchers use to gather people's life stories: interviews and **prompts** to get written stories. Next, you will read about techniques that are used to make sense of those stories. Much like in the previous chapter, you'll be able to try out these techniques yourself, both the ones to gather stories and the ones to analyze stories.

> **Prompts** In the context of narrative identity research, instructions that are meant to get people to write (or talk) about particular topics or themes.

How to get the stories: Interviews and prompts

To examine narrative identity, you need to gather people's stories. Stories are detailed personal accounts so they can't be accessed through a multiple-choice survey measure like some of the ones that we discussed in the previous chapter. Not everyone is similarly eager to share their

DOI: 10.4324/9781003557593-11

stories, or they may not know where to start. Therefore, protocols are needed to get to the kind of information that is needed for the study of narrative identity. Both interviews and written prompts can work for that, but research on narrative identity started with an interview.

Life Story Interview

The interview that McAdams developed to conduct the first research on narrative identity is called the **Life Story Interview**, and the most recent version is the Life Story Interview II (McAdams, 2007). You can access it directly from the researcher's website (see the link in "Further sources" at the end of this chapter). The interview questions are predetermined with only a few suggestions for when to ask follow-up questions. This means that the Life Story Interview is best described as a structured interview.

> **Life Story Interview** A comprehensive structured interview that is used to gather insights into people's narrative identity.

In the first part of the interview, people are asked to think of their life as a book with chapters, which is consistent with the idea that a narrative identity has scenes and plots. You might have seen autobiographies like the ones of former U.S. President Barack Obama or Nobel Peace Prize laureate Malala Yousafzai, both of which had hundreds of pages. That's great for books, but it would give researchers headaches and nightmares to be confronted with dozens of book-length life stories. Therefore, people who are interviewed are asked to keep it to two to seven chapters of their life.

In the next part of the interview, the focus is on eight key scenes. These are: a high point; low point; turning point; positive childhood memory; negative childhood memory; vivid adult memory; wisdom event (a scene in which you think you displayed wisdom); and a religious, spiritual, or mystical experience. Given that there's a vivid adult memory scene, it isn't hard to see that the interview is meant for adults. This reflects the idea that it's mainly by young adulthood (your 20s) that a narrative identity becomes a central part of your personality, which is not to say that adolescents or even children don't already have elements of a narrative identity (McAdams & Olson, 2010). One thing that you can do as you try to make sense of the use of these key scenes is to think about a positive childhood memory and high point for yourself. What comes to mind? Think for a little bit about why those scenes come to mind before you read on. If you're struggling to come up with something, look up the full question that participants get in the interview using the link in the "Further sources" section of this chapter!

The next sections of the Life Story Interview cover participants' thoughts on their future, challenges they have encountered, and their personal ideology. All those sections have subsections, too, which illustrates how thorough the interview is: it truly gets to a lot of information about a person's life! The questions it uses are detailed to make sure that participants do respond in the intended way. Consider for example the first part of the section on personal ideology. There, the instructions are as follows:

> *Now, I would like to ask a few questions about your fundamental beliefs and values and about questions of meaning and morality in your life. Please give some thought to each of these questions.*
>
> *Consider for a moment the religious or spiritual aspects of your life. Please describe in a nutshell your religious beliefs and values, if indeed these are important to you. Whether you are religious or not, please describe your overall ethical or moral approach to life* (McAdams, 2007, p. 5).

This illustrates that some of the questions are rather specific. However, the interview also gets to more general identity aspects, such as the sense of **coherence** that an identity is supposed to provide (see Chapter 1), as in the "Life Theme" section where participants are asked to find a central thema across all the story parts they told. It's not always easy for participants themselves to find consistent themes throughout the interview responses, but researchers search for such themes as well. What that can look like will be covered later, but let's first look at some advantages and disadvantages of the interview.

> **Coherence** In the context of narrative identity research, whether a story is told in a logical way. It could, for example, refer to whether earlier events are logically linked to later events.

An obvious advantage of the interview is its thoroughness. Lots of important information can be gathered, making it possible to obtain a detailed account of what is relevant to someone's identity. The very last section of the interview even gives participants the chance to bring up themes that weren't covered yet! That thoroughness is also related to one of the downsides: the interview can take up to two hours, so much like with the Identity Status Interview (see Chapter 7) it is hard to gather data from large numbers of people. It is partly for that reason that alternative methods have been developed to get similar, but less comprehensive, information. The most common of those are prompts for asking people to write about parts of their life story.

Prompts for written narratives

If you want to obtain life stories by asking people to write about them, it's important to provide specific instructions. Otherwise, they might not know where to start or perhaps they might all have a different take on the assignment you gave them, either of which would make you end up with less useful information. This is more of a problem with written narratives compared to an interview, as you don't have the opportunity to ask follow-up questions. What you need for written narratives are good prompts. Fortunately, those are available.

There are commonly used prompts for several key scenes featured in the Life Story Interview, like high points, low points, and turning points. Other widely used prompts include ones for self-defining memories. The one below was used by McLean (2004) and adapted from earlier work (Singer & Blagov, 2002):

Definition of a self-defining memory

A self-defining memory is a personal memory that has the following attributes:

1. It is at least 1 year old.
2. It is a memory of a specific event in your life that you remember very clearly and that still feels important to you even as you think about it now.
3. It is a memory that helps you to understand who you are as an individual and might be the memory you would tell someone else if you wanted that person to understand you in a more profound way.
4. It may be a memory that is positive or negative, or both, in how it makes you feel. The only important aspect is that it leads to strong feelings.
5. It is a memory that you have thought about many times. It should be familiar to you like a picture you have studied or a song (happy or sad) you have learned by heart.

To understand best what a self-defining memory is, imagine you have just met someone you like very much and you are going for a long walk together. Each of you is very committed to helping the other get to know the "Real You" . . . In the course of conversation, you describe several memories that you feel convey powerfully how you have come to be the person you currently are. It is precisely these memories that constitute self-defining memories.

Task

On the next three pages, please jot down a caption or one-sentence summary for each of three self-defining memories that come to mind. Then describe each memory with enough detail to help your imagined friend see and feel as you did. Although these memories will be kept confidential, please do not reveal memories that are so painful as to make you feel uncomfortable describing them.

Memory #1

Caption ________________________________

(a brief sentence to identify the event)

My age at the time of the original event ___

Other person/persons involved in the event________________

Description of the event: where you were, whom you were with, what happened, how you and others reacted. Include details that will help an imagined friend see and feel as you did.

Note. The last part of the prompt is repeated for the second and third memory.

As you can see, the instructions are detailed especially regarding the definition of a self-defining memory. Because of this, the use of prompts in narrative identity research does tend to give researchers the information they want. As a researcher who has used prompts like this (but then for turning points, translated to Dutch), I frequently got feedback from participants on how responding to those prompts can feel almost therapeutic. This is for similar reasons to why people keep diaries and why therapists sometimes even recommend keeping those! To better understand how these prompts work, you can try and respond to this one yourself. You could write something as short as a paragraph, but write as much as you like! If you write a story, it may come in handy in the next section, where coding will be discussed.

Making sense of stories: Coding

Coding was already briefly mentioned in Chapter 7, but to repeat and then elaborate on what was written there: it is the process of categorizing data before doing analyses. Coding can be applied to both quantitative and qualitative data, and the resulting codes can also be used for either quantitative or qualitative analyses. In other words, it is possible to quantify qualitative data and then do statistical analyses. However, that isn't always the desired way of doing things! What the best option is depends on your research question.

In narrative identity research, where you do start out with written or spoken language as data, both quantitative and qualitative coding have been used. An example of qualitative coding in narrative identity research comes from a study on ethnic-racial identity narratives of Black and Latinx college students at a university in the Midwest part of the United States (Rosario et al., 2023). The researchers conducting this study had several goals, one of which was to investigate how students navigated racial experiences they encountered at their university.

One example of racial experiences was for students to find others who had similar lived experiences as they did. If you're part of a majority group like I was when I grew up, then the importance of this may not be immediately obvious because you'd constantly be surrounded by people with similar lived experiences. However, if you're part of a marginalized group (a group that's not necessarily literally a minority, but one whose members face discrimination based on being considered part of that group, see also Chapter 4) the importance of this will likely be clear. Another example referred to experiences of discrimination in the form of microaggressions, which are "commonly occurring, brief, verbal or nonverbal, behavioral, and environmental indignities that communicate derogatory attitudes or notions toward a different 'other'" (American Psychological Association, n.d.). They can be intentional or unintentional, but regardless of the perpetrators' intention they can be harmful.

Rosario and colleagues examined how and what students learned about themselves and/or their relationships based on these experiences. In other words, their focus was on **meaning making**. Within meaning making, they distinguished seven codes, such as "belonging" and "exploration". They then

> **Meaning making** In the context of narrative identity research, how individuals make sense of their experiences and what they learned about themselves and/or their relationships based on these experiences.

provided definitions of these codes and illustrated them with examples taken from their interviews. Such interview quotes are referred to as **excerpts**. This is an excerpt for the "exploration" code:

Excerpt Passages taken from a source. In the context of identity research, often an interview quote to illustrate a code or theme.

> *Understanding my position at this school, understanding what power I hold as a Black male, as a cisgender*[1] *Black male, and how to use the resources, however many or however few, that disclose for letting me with to better my own living, to help other people out and better represent the communities that I hold dearly to myself* (Rosario et al., 2023, p. 116 and 120).

You probably get the idea of qualitative coding now: no number is assigned to particular occurrences in the interview. If you use quantitative coding of qualitative data, you do assign a number. In the context of narrative identity research, you would assign a particular number to a story on a certain topic of interest. For example, there has been a longstanding interest in **agency**. The relative presence or absence of evidence for a person being agentic can then be coded by assigning a number on a rating scale, such as the one described in the coding manual developed by Adler (n.d.). A slightly edited version of this coding manual is provided in the textbox below.

Agency The feeling that you have some sense of control over your own life.

Narratives high in agency are fundamentally concerned with the autonomy of the protagonist. Highly agentic narratives describe protagonists who can affect their own lives, initiate changes on their own, and who achieve some degree of control over the course of their experiences. This theme is related to the degree to which people internalize their actions and engage in them with a full sense of choice. This achievement may come through self-insight, gaining a sense of control, or a feeling of increased power. The theme of agency bears some relationship to internal locus of control, but it is not identical; for example, if someone feels that they are responsible for everything in their life, but they are failing at all of them, they might be rated as high in internal locus of control, but low in agency. This theme should be coded only as it pertains to the protagonist of the narrative, not other characters.

Code 0–4, where 4 = highest agency

0. Protagonist is completely powerless, at mercy of circumstances; all action is motivated by external powers; or narrative is not written in first person (rare).
1. Protagonist is somewhat at the mercy of circumstances, with primary control of the plot at the hands of external powers.
2. Recorded where there is no code-able language pertaining to the theme of agency (quite rare), or when narrative displays equal amounts of both agentic and nonagentic elements.
3. Protagonist is minimally at the mercy of circumstances, with the majority of the control of the plot in the hands of the protagonist.
4. Protagonist is agentic, able to affect their own life, initiate changes on their own, and achieves some degree of control over the course of their experiences; may or may not include description of some struggle to achieve agentic status.

Redemption A sequence in which someone gets to a positive outcome after initially experiencing something negative.

There are coding manuals for many more things, such as **redemption** (a sequence in which someone gets to a positive outcome after initially experiencing something negative) or coherence (for example whether earlier events are logically linked to later events; for more examples, see McAdams & McLean, 2013). The actual manuals usually are also longer, as they typically also contain examples of what qualifies for a particular score. Such examples often are also included in the resulting publications. For example, Adler (2012, p. 374) provided the following illustration for an excerpt that qualified as a score of 0:

As my life continues to unravel, I feel the therapy is the only thing that's keeping me together in a positive, goal-oriented way, as opposed to alcohol, which, despite its wonderful and quick way of making me cope with things, has the potential for negative effects.

This next excerpt would qualify as a score of 4 (Adler, 2012; p. 374):

Being on my own is a scary place. At times, I feel like a little kid going somewhere for the first time—exciting, frustrating, wonderful, and scary all at once. These are a lot of changes in my life. I was feeling completely at their mercy, but now I see that I do have control. It's up to me to be able to stick with it and I will rise.

What you could do now is try to code one of your own narratives if you wrote those (for prompts, see earlier in this chapter). Alternatively, you can find yourself an autobiography, song lyrics, or something else that seems autobiographical. If you have someone else code the same narrative, you might find you disagree on your scores. Similarly, there isn't always agreement in qualitative coding. If you disagree, one of you could be wrong, both of you could be wrong, and/or the codebook is not clear enough. To figure out what the problem is you need to discuss the codes you got. There are many things that could be discussed, which may make the process seem overwhelming. Fortunately, there are guidelines.

Syed and Nelson (2015) describe such guidelines, applied to the whole process including how to decide on what you'd specifically want to code and how, on training coders, and on ways to calculate reliability. For example, there often are multiple people coding the same narratives, at least in a part of the sample (e.g., 20%, although that's not enough if it's a small sample; Syed & Nelson, 2015). Other researchers have all their narratives coded by teams of two or three different people per narrative, but with different teams who all handle part of the work. In those situations, you have to make sure that the teams get switched up, because if you don't do that you might run into something called coder drift. That is a phenomenon in which people (or teams of coders) gradually develop their own unique interpretation of the codebook, different from the thing all coders agreed on in the training (Syed & Nelson, 2015). Long story short: coding isn't easy! It is worth the trouble though as research using coded narratives has led to important insights in, for example, mental health and professional development (see Chapters 10 and 11).

Conclusion

In this chapter, you learned about the complex process of gathering and coding data on narrative identity. Along the way, the chapter covered multiple steps in the process and pointed to the use of both interviews and prompts to gather narratives. In addition, examples were provided for coding the data qualitatively and quantitatively. I hope you also took the opportunity to try out some of the methods presented in this chapter! The approaches presented in this chapter are all part of the broader narrative identity approach and complement those presented fitting with the broader identity formation approach (see Chapter 7). The approaches that are discussed in the next chapter are a bit different in that sense as they address more specific parts of identity.

Note

1 A cisgender individual is someone "whose gender identity aligns with their sex assigned at birth. A cisgender man or cisgender woman is thus one whose internal gender identity matches, and presents itself in accordance with, the externally determined cultural expectations of the behavior and roles considered appropriate for one's assigned sex as male or female." (APA, n.d.)

Further sources

1. The Life Story Interview – II: https://cpb-us-e1.wpmucdn.com/sites.northwestern.edu/dist/4/3901/files/2020/11/The-Life-Story-Interview-II-2007.pdf

   If you want to see the whole interview guide for the most recent version of the whole Life Story Interview that you read about in this chapter, then please follow this link to a pdf version of it. It is posted on the website of the researcher (and professor) who developed it, Dr Dan P. McAdams. If the link stops working (sometimes things move!) then just try a web search for The Life Story Interview – II.

2. McLean, K. C. (2016). *The co-authored self: Family stories and the construction of personal identity*. Oxford University Press.

   A very accessible book that nicely illustrates what can be learned about identity development when you use the kind of methodology described in this chapter. It covers how people's personal identities aren't just constructed by themselves, but in a social environment.

3. Syed, M., & Nelson, S. C. (2015). Guidelines for Establishing Reliability When Coding Narrative Data. *Emerging Adulthood*, *3*, 375–387.

   If you like to learn about coding narratives, then this is an important article. It provides an accessible introduction to the type of considerations you need to make when you're coding. I had my undergraduate students read this after I recruited them to code large numbers of narratives back in The Netherlands.

References

Adler, J. M. (n.d). *Revised Coding System for Agency and Communion.* https://cpb-us-e1.wpmucdn.com/sites.northwestern.edu/dist/4/3901/files/2020/11/Revised-Coding-System-for-Agency-and-Communion-developed-by-Jon-Adler.pdf

Adler, J. M. (2012). Living into the story: Agency and coherence in a longitudinal study of narrative identity development and mental health over the course of psychotherapy. *Journal of Personality and Social Psychology, 102*, 367–389. https://doi.org/10.1037/a0025289

American Psychological Association. (n.d.). Cisgender. In *APA dictionary of psychology*. Retrieved June 6, 2025, from https://dictionary.apa.org/cisgender

American Psychological Association. (n.d.). Microaggression. In *APA dictionary of psychology*. Retrieved June 5, 2025, from https://dictionary.apa.org/microaggression

McAdams, D. P. (1985). *Power, intimacy, and the life story: Personological inquiries into identity*. Guilford Press.

McAdams, D. P. (2007). *The Life Story Interview – II.* Northwestern University, Evanston, IL. Retrieved from https://cpb-us-e1.wpmucdn.com/sites.northwestern.edu/dist/4/3901/files/2020/11/The-Life-Story-Interview-II-2007.pdf

McAdams, D. P., & McLean, K. C. (2013). Narrative Identity. *Current Directions in Psychological Science*, *22*, 233–238. https://doi.org/10.1177/0963721413475622

McAdams, D. P., & Olson, B. D. (2010). Personality development: Continuity and change over the life course. *Annual Review of Psychology, 61*, 517–542. https://doi.org/10.1146/annurev.psych.093008.100507

McLean, K. C. (2004). *Meaning-making and functions of memory telling in late adolescents' self-defining memory narratives.* Unpublished doctoral dissertation, University of California, Santa Cruz, CA.

Rosario, R. J., Moffitt, U., & Rogers, L. O. (2023). "Where's My People?": An Investigation of the Structure and Content of Black and Latinx College Students' Ethnic-Racial Identity Narratives. *Emerging Adulthood, 12*, 110–127. https://doi.org/10.1177/21676968231214020

Singer, J. A. & Blagov, P. (2002). *Self Defining Memory Request & Rating Sheet.* Connecticut College, New London, CT. Retrieved from http://www.self-definingmemories.com/SDM_Request___Rating_Sheet.pdf

Syed, M., & Nelson, S. C. (2015). Guidelines for Establishing Reliability When Coding Narrative Data. *Emerging Adulthood*, *3*, 375–387. https://doi.org/10.1177/2167696815587648

Chapter 9

Measuring specific aspects of identity

The previous two chapters focused on measures relevant to two broad and widely applied approaches in research on identity development: the identity formation approach and the narrative identity approach. Much of what these measures get to are processes such as exploration and commitment, and tendencies that are identity-relevant such as experiencing agency, redemption, and coherence. These measures do not directly get to more specific issues such as what specific people consider the most important parts of their identity, how they manage relationships between the different parts of their identity, and what kind of stress they experience related to identity matters. Measures for these issues will be covered in this chapter, starting with those that relate to the "what" of identity.

Measuring the "what" of identity

If someone feels a strong commitment to being an antisocial person or feels a high sense of agency in their antisocial actions, then that's typically not considered a good thing. In other words, it is important to know what people are strongly committed to or what they feel agentic about. For that reason, measures addressing what people consider important to who they are, are equally important as those addressing identity processes. Two measures that get to this "what" of identity are discussed below.

The Twenty Statements Test

Research on narrative identity as described in the previous chapter can give some insights into what is important to people when they describe themselves. However, narratives or stories might only reveal part of is important to someone's sense of identity. A more direct and quicker way to examine what someone's identity consists of is provided by a measure called

DOI: 10.4324/9781003557593-12

the **Twenty Statements Test** (Kuhn & McPartland, 1954). It is a questionnaire, but of a somewhat unusual kind as it is a sentence-completion task. This means that research participants are asked to complete a statement starting with "I am . . ." up to 20 times. That's a lot, so I'll ask you to do this just 5 times:

> **Twenty Statements Test** A measure in which people are asked to complete a sentence starting with "I am . . ." twenty times. It can be used to assess someone's identity content (the "what" of one's identity).

1. *I am*...
2. *I am*...
3. *I am*...
4. *I am*...
5. *I am*...

The first thing you could do now is compare your responses to those of others. You'll likely see that everyone is at least somewhat unique in how they complete the statements, but sometimes we also mean the same thing as others and just use different words. To make sense of all those somewhat unique but sometimes similar responses, there are coding procedures to identify broader categories. Johnson and colleagues (2022) used such a procedure called inductive content analysis. That is a form of qualitative coding but given the rather brief responses to the I am-statements there is much less interpretation involved than in the qualitative coding for narrative identity discussed in the previous chapter.

Johnson and colleagues (2022) identified four broad categories: personal, social categories, relationships, and self-evaluation. Within those broad categories there were specific subcodes, with personal characteristics (self-descriptions like "I am funny") within the broad "personal" category being by far the most common. Social categories referred to things like gender, race, or sexual orientation. Relationships referred to friendships, but also to pets, or spiritual relationships, for example with God. Finally, self-evaluation refers to whether people referred to themselves positively ("I am the best"), negatively ("I am not always happy with myself"), or more neutrally. Try to examine in which main categories your I am-statements fit the best!

Obviously, I didn't describe all the details of the study here. Those are available in the full paper by Johnson et al. (2022) linked in the reference list. Keep in mind that their findings apply to adolescents in the United States in 2015, and research conducted in South Africa that considered a broader age range but used the same I am-statements did suggest some age differences. Compared to adolescents, people in their early 20s emphasized relationship qualities more and individual characteristics less (Naudé, 2022).

Intuitively, it would make sense that what people mention in their first I am-statement would be what is the most important to them. However, that's not necessarily the case. To get more insight into how important different parts of people's identities are to them, there is the measure discussed in the next section.

The Aspects of Identity Questionnaire

The purpose of the **Aspects of Identity Questionnaire** (AIQ; Cheek & Cheek, 2018) is pretty straightforward: it simply asks how important a series of identity aspects are to people. For this purpose, the AIQ has the kind of multiple-choice format you read about before. Specifically, it has a response scale ranging from 1 ("not important to my sense of who I am") to 5 ("extremely important to my sense of who I am"). It typically has 35 items divided across the four subscales of personal identity orientation, relational identity orientation, public identity orientation, and collective identity orientation, but additional items are available. Table 9.1 contains examples of aspects of identity that participants rate on their importance.

Aspects of Identity Questionnaire (AIQ) A measure with a multiple-choice format that is used to assess how important four different identity orientations are to the participant: their personal, relational, public, and collective identity orientation.

Table 9.1 Example items of the AIQ (Cheek & Cheek, 2018)

Orientation	*Example Item*
Personal identity	"My personal goals and hopes for the future"
Relational identity	"My commitment to being a concerned relationship partner"
Public identity	"My reputation, what others think of me"
Collective identity	"My feeling of belonging to my community"

Note: A full list of items is available if you follow the QR link below.

There are multiple statements for each of the orientations and if you follow the QR link you can calculate an average score for each of those for yourself. Researchers use those averages to get an idea of whether some orientations are more important to an individual's overall sense of identity than others, or whether particular people derive a sense of identity from a mix of orientations. If you calculate identity orientation scores for yourself, you can examine whether you are strongly drawn to one or multiple identity orientations.

Several studies (e.g., Meca et al., 2015) suggest that the current (fourth) edition of the AIQ has good reliability. It also seems valid as, for example, shown in research by Cheek and Cheek (2018). They compared students from individualistic cultures like the ones that are dominant in North America and Western Europe, to those from more collectivistic cultures with less of a focus on individual achievement and more on things that benefit the community such as cooperation. Students from more collectivistic cultures tended to have higher scores on the collective identity orientation, but not on other orientations, compared to students from more individualistic cultures. This is exactly what would be expected if the measure works in the intended way and therefore suggests the measure is valid. Overall, the AIQ is a useful measure for making sense of how important the broader pieces are within a person's identity puzzle. If you want to know what people do to fit those pieces together, especially when that is a challenge, you'd need the measure described in the next section.

Measuring identity conflicts and tensions and strategies to navigate these

To assess the conflicts and tensions that people often mention when they talk about aspects of their identity, Galliher and colleagues (2025) developed the **Identity Negotiation Experiences and Strategies** (INES) scale. When researchers make a questionnaire, they typically have a theoretical idea and then start constructing their items

Identity Negotiation Experiences and Strategies (INES) A measure with a multiple-choice format that is used to assess someone's identity negotiation experiences and strategies. It has four subscales called strain, vigilance, compartmentalization, and resources.

based on that theory. The researchers who constructed the INES also worked from a theoretical idea but had a somewhat unique approach in that they first gathered input from young people in their late teens and early 20s, for whom the questionnaire was intended. For this purpose, so-called **focus group interviews** were used. Simply put, those are group interviews with one or more people being moderators. The moderator's task is to make all participants feel comfortable and then ask questions about the topic of interest, in this case identity negotiation. These focus group interviews brought up several strategies for dealing with identity issues, including ones that would not have been predicted by theory alone. This information was then directly used to construct questionnaire items, alongside questionnaire items that were based on previous research and theorizing.

Focus group interviews Interviews in which a group of individuals simultaneously participate, so it looks like a group meeting. At least one person is a moderator, who makes all participants comfortable and then asks questions about the topic of interest. The group members then respond.

Initially, this process led to there being 93 items in total. As that's a lot, the researchers used a statistical technique called **factor analysis** to examine whether they could get to the same information with fewer items. Simply put, factor analyses show to which groups of items participants tend to respond in similar ways. For the INES, an example would be the two items "I try to change aspects of my identity so they are accepted by others" and "I prioritize aspects of my identity based on who I am around". Those two items don't get to the exact same issue but do address the same broader topic. Now imagine that your research participants respond to those two items and a couple more that are similar to those in a consistent way. So, if they score high on one, then they'd also be likely to score high on the other ones similar to it, and if they score low on one, they'd also be likely to score low on the other ones similar to it. If that'd be the case, you may have identified a factor. In other words, a factor represents a group of items to which people tend to respond in consistent ways.

Factor analysis Complex statistical technique that uses information based on responses from large groups of people to examine how questionnaire items group together in so-called factors. Those factors are groups of items to which research participants tend to respond in similar ways.

Table 9.2 Example items of the INES (Galliher et al., 2025)

Subscale	*Example item*
Strain	"I often wonder if the different parts of myself will ever fit together"
Vigilance	"I am selective with who I talk about my identity with"
Compartmentalization	"I often adapt my identity depending on how people think I should be"
Resources	"Self-reflection helps me make sense of my identity"

Note: A full list of items is available if you follow the QR link below.

If there are a lot of items that are part of one such factor, then you can probably eliminate a few of those without losing much information. Paired with some other criteria to see whether items would be redundant, this helped the researchers to get the number of items down to 24, so about a quarter of the initial 93. Those 24 items were grouped into four factors that all represented a specific topic within the broader process of identity negotiation. Therefore, those factors also served as the subscales of the questionnaire. They were named "strain", "vigilance", "resources", and "compartmentalization". In Table 9.2, you'll find example items for each of those subscales. By completing the full measure (see QR code below), you can check which identity negotiation strategies you use and which experiences you've had.

The INES is a valid measure according to several criteria. The items were directly derived from experiences of students attending universities in Finland, The Netherlands, and the United States who were dealing with identity negotiation issues, as well as from previous theorizing. The measure's **content validity,** indicating whether a measure covers everything that is relevant to what it intends to measure, is therefore good. The researchers (Galliher et al., 2025) also examined the correlations of the INES subscales with a variety of other identity measures, including the DIDS and the Identity Styles Inventory (see Chapter 7) and the Identity Distress Survey (see next section of this

Content validity Whether a measure covers what are thought to be the most important parts of the construct it is intended to measure.

> **Discriminant validity** Whether a measure of something (for example identity negotiation experiences and strategies) assesses something unique. Examined by assessing whether it is not strongly related to a measure of happiness, or even of different aspects of identity like commitment.

> **Convergent validity** Whether there is relationship between the scores on one measure to scores on another measure that is supposed to assess something similar. For example, the scores on a measure of ruminative exploration should at least be somewhat related to the scores on a measure of worry.

chapter). As the INES didn't measure the exact same thing as those other identity measures, it had good **discriminant validity** as well; it measured something unique (Jordan & Hoeffer, 2011). Yet, the subscales were still correlated with those measures in ways that made sense. For example, people who experienced more strain were also more likely to have higher levels on the similar, but slightly different, construct of ruminative exploration. That all points to good **convergent validity**. Finally, it seems to have good reliability. All in all, the INES seems to work as intended.

Measuring identity-specific distress

This book points to the importance of identity development, but making identity-relevant choices can be overwhelming. The links between identity development and symptoms of psychopathology such as anxiety are covered in a variety of chapters, but there is also stress and worry related to specific identity issues, such as one's career choice or religion[1]. For that kind of stress and worry, the **Identity Distress Survey** was developed (IDS; Berman et al., 2004).

> **Identity Distress Survey (IDS)** A measure with a multiple-choice format that is used to assess someone's level of identity distress about seven broader identity-relevant topics.

Identity distress has been recognized as a diagnosable issue by the **American Psychiatric Association (APA**; Berman et al., 2004) but not everyone experiences identity distress to a degree that warrants therapy. The IDS can also capture the less severe forms of distress that almost everyone experiences at some point. You may have experienced some of this yourself as there are a lot of possible paths in life! Even if you have clear preferences for who or what you'd like to become, there may be challenges getting there. This could be because of structural barriers, as not everyone gets the same opportunities due to systemic inequality. A specific manifestation of such structural issues could be related to sexual orientation, as anything other than heterosexuality isn't always accepted, because of attitudes held by large numbers of people or even laws. It could also be because the path you'd like to follow is one that involves getting into a selective program like medical school. Long story short: there are multiple reasons for experiencing identity-related distress.

American Psychiatric Association The largest American association for psychiatrists. Influential worldwide as they publish one of the most used diagnostic systems for mental disorders, the *Diagnostic and Statistical Manual of Mental Disorders* (DSM).

The first seven items of the IDS cover the same issues that were recognized by the APA as causing identity distress, which contributes to the measure's good content validity. To examine the full range of possible distress levels, the measure has a scale from 1 to 5, running from no distress at all through mild to very severe distress. The last three items cover the impact and severity of the overall distress. You'll find all the items if you follow the QR code link.

In addition to its good content validity, studies conducted in countries around the world have shown that the IDS also has good convergent validity as its scores are associated with those from measures of related identity constructs in the expected way. For example, a study in Poland showed that people with high levels of distress also have low self-esteem (Janowicz et al., 2024). Several studies also point to the measure's

> **Test-retest reliability** If you administer the same measure twice to assess something that is supposed to be somewhat stable across time and your findings suggest it is, then you have good test-retest reliability. Keep in mind that "stable" here means that the higher scoring people on the first measurement occasion should mostly be among the higher scoring people on the second measurement occasion (and the lowest on the first measurement occasion mostly among the lowest scoring ones on the second measurement occasion).

good **test-retest reliability**. That means that those who are among the higher scoring people on identity distress at one point in time are likely to still be among the higher scoring the next time you test them (at least if that's within a couple of weeks), and the lower scoring people at the first measurement point would then still be among the lower scoring ones.

Much like with the other measures, I'd encourage you to complete this measure yourself. It can be helpful to reflect on whether you've ever experienced distress, even if it's just a little bit, related to any of the issues covered by the measure. I have and so have most people! In other words, identity distress is a common and normal part of life. Of course, when the distress is severe and continuously interferes with your daily life it is important to reach out for help.

Conclusion

The measures we covered in this chapter and the previous chapters are commonly used, or have been developed recently. This list is not complete, as basically anything identity related can be measured. For example, the identity motives that were discussed in Chapter 5 can also be measured (see Easterbrook & Vignoles, 2012). However, those motives are one example of constructs that are measured in (slightly) different ways in different studies. Another example is identity control theory, for which researchers typically don't measure the associated constructs directly. Instead, they use experiments to examine whether they can find evidence supporting the theory (see for example Kerpelman & Pittman, 2001). So, while Chapters 7, 8, and this chapter covered quite a few identity measures and measurement approaches, there are still more!

Throughout, this chapter and the previous ones also covered several measurement concepts like several types of validity and reliability. If you are interested in measures beyond the ones that were covered, either for other aspects of identity or something completely different, be critical towards their quality and try applying some of the knowledge on validity and reliability that you obtained. Critical reflection on the quality of our measures is also important in the next section of the book, where key impacts on research, practice, and policy are discussed. After all, good recommendations for the public can only be made based on good science.

Note

1 The focus on specific issues makes this different from ruminative exploration as covered by the DIDS (see Chapter 7), which covers worry about general future plans that are not specific to a particular issue.

Further sources

1. Johnson, S. K., Odjakjian, K., & Park, Y. (2022). I am whatever I say I am: The salient identity content of U.S. adolescents. *Journal of Research on Adolescence, 32*, 737–755. https://doi.org/10.1111/jora.12721

   If you want to read more about how U.S. adolescents complete the sentence "I am . . .", so how they describe what is important to their identity, then this is a pretty accessible academic article on that. Compare your own answers to what you read in the article!

2. Sorgente, A., Claxton, S., Schwab, J., & Vosylis, R. (Eds.). (2025). *Flourishing as a Scholar: Research Methods for the Study of Emerging Adulthood*. Oxford University Press.

   A book in which a wide range of research methods for the study of "emerging adults" (people in between ages 18 and 30-ish) are discussed. There is a heavy focus on identity research in this age group, so if you want to learn more about specific research methods this is a good book to consult!

References

Berman, S. L., Montgomery, M. J., & Kurtines, W. M. (2004). The development and validation of a measure of identity distress. *Identity, 4*, 1–8. https://doi.org/10.1207/S1532706XID0401_1

Cheek, N. N., & Cheek, J. M. (2018). Aspects of identity: From the inner-outer metaphor to a tetrapartite model of the self. *Self and*

Identity, 17, 467–482. https://doi.org/10.1080/15298868.2017.1412347

Easterbrook, M., & Vignoles, V. L. (2012). Different groups, different motives: Identity motives underlying changes in identification with novel groups. *Personality and Social Psychology Bulletin, 38*(8), 1066–1080. https://doi.org/10.1177/0146167212444614

Galliher, R. V., Parmenter, J. G., Pradell, L. R., & Klimstra, T. (2025). Development and validation of the identity negotiation experiences and strategies scale. *Identity, 25*, 373–391. https://doi.org/10.1080/15283488.2024.2377171

Janowicz, K., Ciesielski, P., Ćwiklińska, J., & Piasecka, A. (2024). Polish version of the Identity Distress Survey: Reliability, factor structure, validity, relationships with mental health. *European Review of Applied Psychology/Revue Européenne de Psychologie Appliquée, 74*, 100908. https://doi.org/10.1016/j.erap.2023.100908

Johnson, S. K., Odjakjian, K., & Park, Y. (2022). I am whatever I say I am: The salient identity content of U.S. adolescents. *Journal of Research on Adolescence, 32*, 737–755. https://doi.org/10.1111/jora.12721

Jordan, C., & Hoeffer, R. A. (2011). Reliability and validity in quantitative measurement. In: Thyer, B. A. (Ed.). *The Handbook of Social Work Research Methods* (pp. 52–67). Sage. https://doi.org/10.4135/9781412986182

Kerpelman, J. L., & Pittman, J. F. (2001). The instability of possible selves: Identity processes within late adolescent's close peer relationships. *Journal of Adolescence, 24*, 491–512. https://doi.org/10.1006/jado.2001.0385

Kuhn, M. H., & McPartland, T. S. (1954). An empirical investigation of self-attitudes. *American Sociological Review, 19*, 68–76. https://doi.org/10.4324/9781315129945-16

Meca, A., Ritchie, R. A., Beyers, W., Schwartz, S. J., Picariello, S., Zamboanga, B. L., Hardy, S. A., Luyckx, K., Kim, S. Y., Whitbourne, S. K., Crocetti, E., Brown, E. J., & Benitez, C. G. (2015). Identity centrality and psychosocial functioning: A person-centered approach. *Emerging Adulthood, 3*, 327–339. https://doi.org/10.1177/2167696815593183

Naudé, L. (2022). Being me: Content and context in South African adolescents' identity development. *Current Psychology, 41*, 2184–2193. https://doi.org/10.1007/s12144-020-00737-w

Section 4

Key impacts

By the end of this section, you will:

- Be able to describe what is known about the relationship between identity development and mental health and discuss its complexities.
- Know how identity development is related to career development and school transitions.
- Be able to provide examples of how identity development can inform, and be affected by, policy.

DOI: 10.4324/9781003557593-13

Chapter 10

The role of identity in mental health

Most people only think of psychologists as people who treat **mental health** problems. That ignores all the other things that psychologists do, like their work in industry and organizations to increase well-being and performance, in the criminal justice system, and even in the design of parks and buildings. Similarly, a key concept in psychology like identity development has a range of applications. However, the roots of much of what is studied by identity researchers can be traced back to psychotherapists like Freud and Erikson (see Chapter 3). This chapter will turn to what is specifically known about the complex relationship between identity development and mental health. You will also learn about how this knowledge can be, and has been, applied.

Mental health One's state of emotional well-being and psychosocial adjustment. Factors that are typically considered to be important indicators of this are the relative absence or presence of internalizing and externalizing problems, but also include the absence and presence of problematic substance use.

Identity and mental health: How and why they are related

The idea that mental health problems may have something to do with people's struggles in figuring out who they are and where they are going in life, can be traced back to first Freud and then Erikson. In addition, Marcia's elaboration on Erikson's work, including the identity status model (see Chapters 5 and 7), was inspired by an experience in which he saw someone with seemingly severe mental health challenges make a sudden recovery which should not have been possible if they really had the condition with which they were diagnosed (Kroger & Marcia, 2022). Erikson's

DOI: 10.4324/9781003557593-14

(1950/1993) concept of identity confusion provided an explanation for this, perhaps because Erikson had written that identity confusion could be accompanied by "delinquent and outright psychotic episodes" that, if the client received appropriate care, did "not have the same fatal significance they have at other ages" (p. 262). In sum, the study of identity is strongly rooted in the study and treatment of mental health problems. Therefore, it shouldn't come as a surprise that the relationship between identity development and mental health has been studied a lot.

Much of the work on the relationship between identity and mental health has been based on Marcia's identity statuses of achievement, moratorium, foreclosure, and diffusion, and the dimensions underlying those: various forms of commitment and exploration (see also Chapters 5 and 7). Based on research grounded in Marcia's approach involving a large number of studies conducted in a bunch of different countries and age groups, the findings seem pretty straightforward: people who have stronger commitments tend to have "better" mental health outcomes as indicated by, for example, less anxiety and fewer or less severe symptoms of depression (Branje et al., 2021). If that were the whole story, the conclusion would be simple: strong commitments are good for you. However, things are actually much more complicated.

The first thing to keep in mind is that it matters what kind of mental health outcomes and what kind of identity dimensions you are looking at. For example, solid evidence exists for stronger commitment being related to fewer **internalizing problems** and **externalizing problems** (van Doeselaar et al., 2018), and sometimes but not always to less use of substances such as alcohol and marijuana (e.g., de Moor et al., 2022; Ritchie et al., 2013). Internalizing problems include anxiety and depression, whereas externalizing problems include aggression and delinquency. Internalizing and externalizing problems are sometimes also related to exploration dimensions, especially the forms of exploration that are characterized by doubts such as reconsideration and ruminative exploration. There,

Internalizing problems Problems that are directed more "inward". They don't directly affect those around the people who have them, but primarily the person themselves. Examples are anxiety and depression

Externalizing problems Problems that are directed more "outward", in the sense that they can affect other people around those who have them. Examples are aggression and delinquency.

it's higher levels of ruminative exploration or reconsideration that are associated with higher levels of such problems (Crocetti, 2017; Luyckx et al., 2008). For substance use and risk behaviors such as reckless driving, the link with exploration is less clear (de Moor et al., 2022; Ritchie et al., 2013). The reason for this may be that identity exploration can involve experimentation, and there's different types of that. Some types of experimentation may be of the riskier kind, like trying out substances that you aren't allowed to legally use at the age you're at, such as using alcohol in adolescence. Or it could be related to testing the boundaries of your car handling skills when you get your driver's license and finding those by ending up next to the road. Other experimentation may be of a very different kind: entering talent shows for skills you're not sure you have or joining another sports team every month until you find your calling. That kind of experimentation can be associated with the use of fewer substances and fewer risky behaviors. Adding those things up can explain why the link of exploration with risky behaviors isn't all that clear.

A second thing to keep in mind is that even the associations between identity and mental health related issues that are consistently found, aren't all that strong. In other words, not every person with weak commitments is more anxious and depressed. All we know is that if we only have information on a person's commitments and those are weak, then our best guess would be that they likely have somewhat higher rather than lower levels of anxiety and depression. But: it's just a prediction and, much like weather predictions, predictions of levels of psychological variables are far from perfect and don't work for every individual all of the time.

A third thing is that there are a lot of reasons why identity and mental health may be related to each other. Let's just cover a few here (for a longer list, see for example Klimstra & Denissen, 2017), applied to the finding that weak commitments tend to go together with high anxiety as an example. Perhaps the most intuitive explanation for weak commitments and high anxiety being related to each other would be that having weak commitments leads to a sense of insecurity, which in turn triggers anxiety. However, it could also be the other way around, as being anxious might make you reluctant to commit to things ("what if this is not the right choice to make?"). Yet another reason could be what is called a third variable, something that affects both identity commitment and anxiety. In that case, it would look like the two might influence each other, whereas that's not directly the case. Think for example about the threat of losing your job. That will likely lower your commitment and, because of the financial uncertainty it may bring, it would likely trigger some anxiety, too.

Those were just three simple reasons for why the same association might occur, but for all three of those we already have to rely on one assumption: that identity commitment and anxiety are two separate things. You might be like "well, yeah, of course", but think about this a little more. For example, you've probably heard someone describing themselves as anxious. In that case, being an anxious person can be part of their identity. In fact, some people are known to have strong commitments to identity aspects like being anxious or depressed (e.g., Cruwys & Gunaseelan, 2016). Perhaps needless to say, being more committed to an identity as an anxious person would be unlikely to be associated with lower anxiety.

It is also not just commitment and exploration that are related to mental health. For example, research on identity styles has repeatedly shown that the diffuse-avoidant style tends to be associated with poorer mental health (Berzonsky, 2011). Similarly, other broad aspects of identity, such as distinctiveness, are also associated with mental health (van Doeselaar et al., 2018). Higher distinctiveness (feeling more distinguishable from others; see Chapter 1) is associated with positive mental health, but only up to a certain level, as extremely high distinctiveness tends to be associated with poorer mental health. Finally, and it may be somewhat obvious, but identity distress tends to go together with mental health issues as well (Berman & Montgomery, 2014)

In sum, there is evidence for several aspects of identity being related to mental health, but this relationship can be there for many reasons. Keep that in mind the next time you read about this kind of topic or hear someone talking about it.

Identity and the diagnosis of mental health problems

Editions of the ***Diagnostic and Statistical Manual of Mental Disorders*** (DSM) from the distant past included an identity disorder. It was described as a pattern of "severe subjective distress regarding the inability to integrate aspects of the self into a relatively coherent and acceptable sense of self" (Berman et al., 2004, p. 1), related to a range of identity issues, including but not limited to career choice, values, and sexual behavior and orientation. However, by the mid-1990s, it was no longer considered a disorder, but a "potentially

> ***Diagnostic and Statistical Manual of Mental Disorders* (DSM)** A manual containing criteria for when someone meets the requirements of a diagnosis for a mental disorder. It is used by mental healthcare professionals to examine whether their clients should get a diagnosis and what that diagnosis should be. It also provides additional information related to mental disorders, such as their prevalence.

relevant condition" that clinicians might want to pay attention to, and renamed to **"identity problem"**. In other words, it was considered less important, but that didn't stop identity researchers from keeping it in the spotlight. In fact, its existence was a primary reason for the development of the Identity Distress Survey (see Chapter 9).

Identity problem A condition described in the DSM-IV in which a person experiences severe distress because of an "inability to integrate aspects of the self into a relatively coherent and acceptable sense of self" (Berman et al., 2004, p. 1).

Another identity disorder was retained in the DSM: **dissociative identity disorder** (DID). Conditions that would now be called DID have been recognized at least since the 19th century, but for a long time went under different names, such as multiple personality disorder (Dorahy et al., 2014). Key symptoms are "a) the presence of two or more distinct personality states or an experience of possession and b) recurrent episodes of dissociative amnesia" (American Psychiatric Association, 2022). Personality states are temporary so they're not really your actual personality, because your actual personality would be the overall pattern of what you're like across those states. The personality states themselves can be viewed as identities. In DID, the differences between the identities of one person can be so extreme that the autobiographical memories of people with DID in one state are completely different and disconnected from their autobiographical accounts in another state. In other words, people diagnosed with DID may tell you about important life events (for example marriage or graduation) when they are in one state but then are unable to remember any of that when they are in another state and suddenly have a whole set of different memories instead. This is what is meant by the "dissociative amnesia" symptom mentioned earlier. DID is rare; it occurs in only about 1.5% of the population (American Psychiatric Association, 2022). You might have read about it or seen movies about it, but keep in mind that media portrayals of DID aren't all that accurate and they tend to draw on stereotypes that can be damaging for those who live with this condition

Dissociative identity disorder (DID) According to the American Psychiatric Association (2022), a condition characterized by "the presence of two or more distinct personality states or an experience of possession" and "recurrent episodes of dissociative amnesia".

(Snyder et al., 2024). The identity issues associated with DID are rather unique and different in severity from those discussed in the rest of the book. However, it is important to cover because it could be part what people initially think of when they hear the word "identity".

> **Personality disorders** According to the American Psychiatric Association (2022), "an enduring pattern of inner experience and behavior that deviates markedly from the norms and expectations of the individual's culture, is pervasive and inflexible, has an onset in adolescence or early adulthood, is stable over time, and leads to distress or impairment". Ten personality disorders are distinguished in the most recent version of the DSM.

The most recent version of the diagnostic system of the American Psychiatric Association (DSM-5-TR; American Psychiatric Association, 2022) also refers to the role of identity in a whole set of other diagnoses: **personality disorders** (PDs). A PD is defined as:

> an enduring pattern of inner experience and behavior that deviates markedly from the norms and expectations of the individual's culture, is pervasive and inflexible, has an onset in adolescence or early adulthood, is stable over time, and leads to distress or impairment (American Psychiatric Association, 2022).

There are ten different PDs. Some you may have heard of are borderline PD, antisocial PD, and paranoid PD. Those would all be considered diagnostic categories. However, DSM-5-TR PDs also includes an alternative, dimensional, view of PDs. The basic idea there is that we all have some symptoms of PDs, but that for most of us the levels of those symptoms are very low. For treatment to be necessary, the symptoms have to be beyond a certain level, but people under that level aren't completely problem free. There are different sets of symptoms, including deviations in broad tendencies that are relatively stable across time, such as negative affectivity, which is a tendency to experience negative emotions.

A healthy sense of identity is part of another set of symptoms, referred to as personality functioning (American Psychiatric Association, 2022). One aspect of identity mentioned in DSM-5 is typically not referred to as such by identity researchers: normal emotional experiences and emotion regulation. The other two aspects are more widely recognized as parts of identity: experiencing distinctiveness and having stable and positive self-esteem. Similar to how it is described in Chapter 1 of this book, DSM-5 describes problems in distinctiveness as a problem of individuals in not seeing clear boundaries between themselves and others, overidentifying with others, and letting others define who they are (American Psychiatric Association, 2022). Self-esteem refers to an individual's evaluation of their own worth as a person (see Chapter 3). According to DSM-5, one self-esteem issue is having a very negative self-evaluation. Another one is fragile self-esteem, which means that one's self-esteem is easily threatened by external circumstances or by what happens in a particular situation. For example, someone might get one negative comment from a random stranger while they get plenty of positive feedback otherwise. If they still felt completely useless for days just because of that one comment, then that'd be an indication of fragile self-esteem. A third problem, inflated self-esteem, so feeling like you're the best thing that ever happened to the world despite deep down knowing that's not the case, can come with similar issues.

There are specific scales to rate the aspects of identity disturbance recognized in DSM-5, but several researchers have pointed out that the role of identity in PDs is broader. For example, narrative identity (see Chapters 4 and 8) and its development in adolescence are also related to PDs (Shiner et al., 2021). Therapists often already pay attention to the life stories of their clients, so the link to narrative identity makes a lot of sense! Further research also suggests links between symptoms of specific PDs such as borderline with commitment and exploration dimensions (e.g., Bogaerts et al., 2021).

In sum, several aspects of identity covered in this book are associated with PDs. Some of those, such as distinctiveness, are already frequently assessed when PDs are diagnosed. Others, such as aspects of narrative identity or commitment and exploration dimensions, are not. Theoretical accounts have long emphasized the role of identity in a variety of forms of mental health problems, which include personality disorders (Marcia, 2006). Research has even shown that people's narrative identities can change over the course of psychotherapy even when it's not a direct therapy goal (Adler, 2012). All of this suggests that even more can be done with using identity knowledge in the diagnosis and treatment of PDs.

Conclusion

Psychotherapists played a large role in starting the study of identity and its development and this chapter illustrates that the identity-mental health link is clearly there. However, the link is complicated as there are many ways in which the two can be related to each other. Sometimes, they can't even be separated. Perhaps the clearest example of that would be dissociative identity disorder, in which identity problems are the mental health problem. Now that the role of identity issues is increasingly recognized in diagnostic systems, knowledge on the links between identity and mental health is further expanding and increasingly applied in practice. This makes it important to know about these linkages, for mental health professionals and for everyone with an interest in identity.

Further sources

1. What are personality disorders? https://www.psychiatry.org/patients-families/personality-disorders/what-are-personality-disorders

   After reading this chapter you might want to know more about personality disorders. Fortunately, the website of the American Psychiatric Association provides a thoughtful overview.

2. Snyder, B. L., Boyer, S. M., Caplan, J. E., Nester, M. S., & Brand, B. (2024). It's not just a movie: perceived impact of misportrayals of dissociative identity disorder in the media on self and treatment. *European Journal of Trauma & Dissociation*, *8*, 100429.

   There have been lots of movies and other media portrayals that have sensationalized mental health problems such as those associated with dissociative identity disorder. It can be tempting to draw on stereotypes (I am not immune to that tendency!), but, as you can read in this research study, stereotypical and sensationalized portrayals of (severe) mental health problems are damaging and problematic.

References

Adler, J. M. (2012). Living into the story: Agency and coherence in a longitudinal study of narrative identity development and mental health over the course of psychotherapy. *Journal of Personality and Social Psychology*, *102*, 367–389.

American Psychiatric Association. (2022). *Diagnostic and statistical manual of mental disorders* (5th ed., text rev.).

Berman, S. L., & Montgomery, M. J. (2014). Problematic identity processes: The role of identity distress. *Identity*, *14*, 241–245.

Berman, S. L., Montgomery, M. J., & Kurtines, W. M. (2004). The development and validation of a measure of identity distress. *Identity*, *4*, 1–8.

Berzonsky, M. D. (2011). A social-cognitive perspective on identity construction. In: Schwartz, S. J., Luyckx, K., & Vignoles, V. L. (Eds.), *Handbook of identity theory and research* (pp. 55–76). Springer. https://doi.org/10.1007/978-1-4419-7988-9_3

Bogaerts, A., Claes, L., Bastiaens, T., & Luyckx, K. (2021). Personality disorder symptomatology in Belgian emerging adults: Associations with identity processes and statuses. *European Journal of Developmental Psychology*, *18*, 75–95.

Branje, S., De Moor, E. L., Spitzer, J., & Becht, A. I. (2021). Dynamics of identity development in adolescence: A decade in review. *Journal of Research on Adolescence, 31*, 908–927.

Crocetti, E., Rubini, M., & Meeus, W. (2008). Capturing the dynamics of identity formation in various ethnic groups: Development and validation of a three-dimensional model. *Journal of Adolescence, 31*(2), 207–222.

Crocetti E. (2017). Identity formation in adolescence: The dynamic of forming and consolidating identity commitments. *Child Development Perspectives, 11* (2), 145–150, https://doi.org/10.1111/cdep.12226

Cruwys, T., & Gunaseelan, S. (2016). "Depression is who I am": Mental illness identity, stigma and wellbeing. *Journal of Affective Disorders, 189*, 36–42.

de Moor, E. L., Sijtsema, J. J., Weller, J. A., & Klimstra, T. A. (2022). Longitudinal links between identity and substance use in adolescence. *Self and Identity, 21*, 113–136. https://doi.org/10.1080/15298868.2020.1818615

Dorahy, M. J., Brand, B. L., Şar, V., Krüger, C., Stavropoulos, P., Martínez-Taboas, A., Lewis-Fernández, R., & Middleton, W. (2014). Dissociative identity disorder: An empirical overview. *Australian & New Zealand Journal of Psychiatry, 48*, 402–417.

Erikson, E. H. (1950/1993). *Childhood and society.* Norton.

Klimstra, T. A., & Denissen, J. J. A. (2017). A theoretical framework for the associations between identity and psychopathology. *Developmental Psychology, 53*, 2052–2065.

Kroger, J., & Marcia, J. E. (2022). Erikson, the identity statuses, and beyond. In: Bamberg, M., Demuth, C., & Watzlawik, M. (Eds.), *The Cambridge Handbook of Identity* (pp. 215–237). Cambridge University Press. https://doi.org/10.1017/9781108755146.012

Luyckx, K., Schwartz, S. J., Berzonsky, M. D., Soenens, B., Vansteenkiste, M., Smits, I., & Goossens, L. (2008). Capturing ruminative exploration: Extending the four-dimensional model of identity formation in late adolescence. *Journal of Research in Personality, 42*, 58–82.

Marcia, J. E. (2006). Ego identity and personality disorders. *Journal of Personality Disorders, 20*, 577–596.

Ritchie, R. A., Meca, A., Madrazo, V. L., Schwartz, S. J., Hardy, S. A., Zamboanga, B. L., . . . & Lee, R. M. (2013). Identity dimensions and related processes in emerging adulthood: Helpful or harmful?. *Journal of Clinical Psychology, 69*, 415–432.

Shiner, R. L., Klimstra, T. A., Denissen, J. J., & See, A. Y. (2021). The development of narrative identity and the emergence of personality disorders in adolescence. *Current Opinion in Psychology, 37*, 49–53.

Snyder, B. L., Boyer, S. M., Caplan, J. E., Nester, M. S., & Brand, B. (2024). It's not just a movie: perceived impact of misportrayals of dissociative identity disorder in the media on self and treatment. *European Journal of Trauma & Dissociation, 8*, 100429.

Chapter 11

Identity and professional development

Even at a very young age, children are often asked what they want to become later in life. This "what do you want to be" is typically just a way of asking what future job they want to have. That was one of the reasons why my family thought it was hilarious when 5-year-old me enthusiastically answered this question with "bald"! For context, my dad and my grandfathers had varying degrees of baldness, which clearly made baldness an important thing to aspire to. So far, I failed at this as there's still quite some hair on my head. The fact that I'm not sad about that illustrates that goals and aspirations can change over time. More importantly, though, this example illustrates that career aspirations are considered important to who we are and want to become. In other words, they are a key part of the identity development process.

Professional development, which could also be referred to as occupational or career development, includes making decisions and evaluations regarding one's education and other career-related issues, and has been of interest to identity researchers for a long time. Erikson (1950/1993) already stated that "The sense of ego identity, then, is the accrued confidence that the inner sameness and continuity prepared in the past are matched by the sameness and continuity of one's meaning for others, as evidenced in the tangible promise of a 'career'" (pp. 261–262).The quotation marks suggest he didn't think a "career" always needed to be something that everyone would consider a job, but it's clear that identity development is very much intertwined with professional development, largely because so many of us spend such a large part of our life working. This chapter covers how research on identity development has contributed to a better understanding of professional development and how this knowledge has been applied. Several future applications will also be covered.

Identity development and school transitions

It is not just at home, but also in school where young children are asked to talk about their career aspiration. After I figured out that wanting

DOI: 10.4324/9781003557593-15

to become bald wasn't considered an appropriate career goal, at school I would mention wanting to become a firefighter, bridge engineer, software engineer, and likely other things I don't remember anymore. You probably had your own list of career plans. While many of those don't work out and just become fun anecdotes, questions about a career direction do come back throughout your school career. They start carrying more weight as you grow older as they start having real-life implications, for example for the type of school you choose. Knowledge on identity development can be, and has been, applied to help people navigate these complex questions.

The way school systems are structured matters for how and when career questions become relevant. The Netherlands, for example, has a tracked secondary school system starting around age 12. Broadly speaking, there are three tracks. The vocational track is the most applied, preparing students for a variety of trades such as car mechanic, sales associate, security officer, animal trainer, and many more. The academic track has a heavy theoretical focus, preparing students for attending university. Somewhat in between those is the professional track. By the end of elementary school, which typically is at age 11 or 12, students get a recommendation for a track from their teachers, based on their overall performance and their results on a standardized test. They then make an initial choice, which is widely thought to have long-lasting implications even though switching tracks is very possible (I did this myself). In addition, there are also different schools to choose from based on ideological denomination (e.g., a specific religion, or non-religious schools), educational philosophy (e.g., "regular", Montessori, Free Schools), and location. There's really a lot to choose from and those choices are identity relevant.

To better understand what challenges students face and what can be done to help them navigate these challenges, researchers have been studying identity development around this transition. This research suggests that those who do more identity exploration regarding school choice in the year before the transition tend to do better in school after the transition, so once they're in secondary school (de Moor & Branje, 2023). It might seem obvious that exploration is helpful because you would know more about what you're getting into, but it's relatively rare to directly demonstrate its benefits given that it's also stressful to compare different options, especially at a younger age like age 10 or 11. To stimulate exploration, it tends to help if parents provide support and show their children that they like and respect them (de Moor et al., 2023). In other words, one way to ease the transition from elementary to secondary school is to involve parents in the educational decision-making process and to give them recommendations on how to be supportive of their children. You may have experienced something like this yourself: it's easier to explore when you feel like your parents support you.

Later in adolescence there's the transition to tertiary education, which includes trade schools, colleges, and universities. At that point, a slightly different form of parental support tends to help: the kind in which parents support their children in making decisions for themselves (Christiaens et al., 2021). This is called **autonomy support**. Interestingly, anxiety also played a positive role. Obviously, being very anxious can be paralyzing, but having some anxiety turned out to be helpful! This is because a mild bit of worry can help for getting you to think ahead, for example about what a new school will be like. In other words, a bit of worry might get you to explore beforehand and therefore make you a bit better prepared.

Autonomy support A form of parental support in which parents support their children in making decisions for themselves.

Fortunately, the importance of identity exploration is recognized and actively encouraged around the transition to tertiary education, as there are orientations where multiple universities promoted their programs or "student for a day" events. To help students commit to an interest once they are in a program, academic counsellors and advisors coach students by asking them about their goals and values, often unintentionally using principles that align with identity theories. By more intentionally applying knowledge on what helps to stimulate identity development, for example by providing autonomy support instead of being too leading in proposing solutions to study-related issues, such services could be further improved.

Outside of formal advising meetings, there's plenty that educational institutions can do, too. For instance, it's not always easy to find people in college who are like you or have had life experiences comparable to yours. This is especially true for students from underrepresented groups, for example based on race and ethnicity. Research on students from a variety of ethnic-racial groups in the United States showed that support from friends and professors was related to having a stronger sense of identity (Azmitia et al., 2013). In other words, universities that provide students with opportunities to build strong supportive relationships with each other and with professors, are supporting their student's identity development.

Identity development and the transition into working life

Once you have the degrees you need, the transition into working life awaits. To smoothen this transition, schools and universities often help students to turn theory into practice by offering internships. Some studies find few, if any, effects of those internships on identity development.

However, specific events during those internships can matter, as identity commitment strength tends to go up after positive experiences and down after negative experiences (Kunnen, 2023). Even the finding that negative experiences weaken commitments can be seen as a good thing, because figuring out that something isn't going to make you happy isn't necessarily bad. In fact, it can push you to switch to something that makes you happier. This is of course not to say that such experiences aren't stressful!

An internship is still temporary, so what happens when people get their first actual job? There is at least some evidence suggesting that ruminative exploration tends to go down around then (den Boer et al., 2026), which may be because landing a job takes away part of the worries around establishing a career. Still, you shouldn't always keep a job no matter what, because people who voluntarily left a job to, for example, take care of children, become an entrepreneur, or go study some more, also experienced decreases in ruminative exploration (Mannerström et al., 2019). The next chapter will cover issues on how such flexibility is not available everywhere and for everyone. However, if unemployment is low or you have the resources to take some risk, a career change can give a positive boost to your identity and with that your well-being.

Other research suggests that exploration before and while you have a job is important, too, as people with weaker commitments who also didn't explore much were at increased risk for developing burnout symptoms related to their job (Luyckx et al., 2010). In terms of the identity statuses (see Chapter 5), even so-called foreclosed individuals, so those who were committed but hadn't explored much before they made their commitments, were less invested in their job than the achieved individuals who had made commitments after exploration. In other words, if you have the opportunity to find a job that you like but that process requires some exploration, that exploration may be worth it. In addition to this, narrative identity development has also been shown to affect how people feel about their job. Specifically, people often attempt to construct agentic narrative identities which emphasize that they have control over what they are doing (Scott, 2022). This is effective, as it can help to make the job feel more meaningful and increase your well-being. So, if employers were to stimulate their employees' commitments and exploration as well as narrative identity development, they'd get happier and less burned-out workers.

The previous paragraph covers examples based on approaches to identity development that were covered in Chapter 4, 5, 7, and 8. However, there's also the concept of **occupational identity**, which refers to

> **Occupational identity** What people see as their work-related interests, abilities, goals, and values, and how they link these to current and possible work roles.

what people see as their work-related interests, abilities, goals, and values, and how they link these to current and possible work roles (Skorikov & Vondracek, 2011). Occupational identity is sometimes also referred to as career identity, professional identity, work identity, vocational identity, or words related to those. If you're interested in further information on that, I recommend reading the book chapter I cited in this paragraph.

Further applications for professional development

In the previous sections, you learned about some of the links between identity development and professional development, and some of the things that have been, or could be, done to stimulate it. There is more, though! Take career orientation programs. These now often help you figure out your interests with standardized assessments that look like personality tests. Follow-up conversations then do focus on why you would want to pursue a particular career direction, which can trigger exploration. That's a good thing as exploration has been shown to be important for school and work adjustment. However, not all types of exploration are always helpful. For example, due to a variety of circumstances (for example a bad economy with few viable career options) people may find themselves with few options to choose from. Comparing lots of different options that turn out be unfeasible would then just be frustrating. In that case, exploration in depth, so for example figuring out what you can do with the study you ended up pursuing, could be the recommended thing to do.

Narrative processing can also be very helpful for figuring out why you're doing what you're doing, or why you want to do what you want to do. If people openly reflect on their autobiographical memories to understand their meaning and impact on their identity, they engage in what is referred to as **exploratory processing.** This does not directly boost their identity exploration or commitment (Turner et al., 2024). However, it does help people to figure out how they navigated past challenges that they see as important, thereby potentially helping them figure out more about what they are like, what is important to them, and what their strengths and limitations are. Also, writing about what made you decide to follow a career direction can help for reminding yourself why you're doing what you're doing.

Exploratory processing The extent to which people openly reflect on their autobiographical memories to understand their meaning and impact on their identity.

In other words, talking or writing about career choices can strengthen your narrative career identity.

Most of us don't work forever, but little is known about the role of identity around retirement. For many of you, retirement will feel like something that's far away and it likely is if you only think of it as stopping working when you're in your late 60s or older. However, for some jobs or roles retirement comes much earlier. Among the best-documented ones are retirement of college-student athletes who don't go on to be professional athletes and the retirement of professional athletes. In the United States, there are many college-student athletes, the vast majority of whom retire from sports when they graduate at age 21 or so because they won't go on to be a professional athlete. Their retirement might not seem like a big deal, but keep in mind that they often spend over 20 hours a week on their sport during the season, and they will have done this in middle and high school, too. Also, some of them play their games in front of large crowds, sometimes over 100,000 people per game. Even at colleges with less prestigious teams, crowds reach 3,000 people or more. Given the large chunk of time it takes up and its popularity, it is perhaps no wonder that retirement can impact mental health negatively (Giannone et al., 2017).

The role of identity in retirement from various roles is not typically studied from the perspective of the theories covered the most in this book. One exception to this is a study showing that exploration was lower in British adults who were beyond retirement age compared to those who were younger than retirement age (Weller et al., 2026). Commitment levels were pretty equal when those who were in their late 60s and older were compared to younger adults. Research literally focusing on retirement, instead of the age around which retirement typically occurs, takes a slightly different approach to identity. It often relies on a concept that is referred to as **role identity** (e.g., Bordia et al., 2020), so it's about what you think you are like in a specific role like a worker or an athlete.

Role identity What you (think) you are like in a specific role, like for example that of an athlete, parent, student, or job role such as teacher.

While having a strong identity typically is a good thing, for college athletes in North America (in this case Canada) who still had a strong athletic identity after they no longer were athletes, it was a risk factor for mental health problems (Giannone et al., 2017). Research on retirement of professional athletes in other parts of the world shows that just dropping your athletic identity altogether isn't a good thing to do either as athletic identity loss was also associated with increased risk for mental health problems (Haslam et al., 2021). However, such risks could be offset by staying in social groups that these athletes were already part of before retirement or by joining new groups after retirement.

If you don't care about athletes, do know that the same principles can be applied to other roles as there are many possible things to spend much of your time on. Some examples are being part of a particular interest group (perhaps addressing a particular topic like climate change), an orchestra, band, or crafts group. For any substantial role that is important to who you are and that at some point stops, it can help to make sure you've got ongoing social support in place that extends beyond that one role. In fact, the same appears to be true for when you retire from a job later in life (Haslam et al., 2018).

In addition to joining new groups, retirement from work also tends to go smoother if you identify as a retiree (Haslam et al., 2018). Retiring people who described themselves as retirees tended to be happier with their retirement and more satisfied with their life. Also, people who had either had strong non-work role identities before retirement or were able to adapt their work role identity into a non-work role identity, tended to have an easier time transitioning into retirement (Bordia et al., 2020). Those who didn't have strong non-work role identities and had a hard time transforming their work role identity into a non-work one struggled the most. This illustrates that it's not just the practical aspects of retirement, such as financial issues, that should be addressed by employers. The psychological aspect of retirement, specifically how people define themselves, so, their identities, should get attention as well.

Conclusion

In sum, the role of identity in professional development has been studied from the end of elementary school all the way to retirement. Various things are known to be helpful for people in navigating decisions and transitions throughout their career. Importantly, while identity development and professional development may intuitively seem like things that are all about you, it isn't helpful to only focus on yourself. Support from people around you is important! Although there is still work to be done to make better use of the knowledge that we already have on identity development, educational institutions and some employers already recognize the importance of identity development. Knowledge on identity development can be, and has been, successfully applied to help people navigate their professional career.

Further sources

1. A Man on The Inside (Season 1). https://www.imdb.com/title/tt26670955/

   Comedy series about a retired professor who is looking for new purpose and meaning in life. He becomes a mole in a case led by a private investigation agency. It can be seen as a funny take on how people deal with professional identity issues.

2. Mean Girls. https://www.imdb.com/title/tt0377092/

   Movie that deals with a lot of things, but centers around the difficulties of making a school transition. Focuses on the role of friendship cliques but also deals with identity issues.

3. Skorikov, V. B., & Vondracek, F. W. (2011). Occupational Identity. In: Schwartz, S., Luyckx, K., & Vignoles, V. (Eds.). *Handbook of Identity Theory and Research*. Springer. https://doi.org/10.1007/978-1-4419-7988-9_29

   Not every further source can be a movie (unfortunately?). Therefore, if you want to know everything about occupational identity, so how we form an identity in the workplace, this chapter offers a great introduction.

References

Azmitia, M., Syed, M., & Radmacher, K. (2013). Finding your niche: Identity and emotional support in emerging adults' adjustment to the transition to college. *Journal of Research on Adolescence, 23*, 744–761. https://doi.org/10.1111/jora.12037

Bordia, P., Read, S., & Bordia, S. (2020). Retiring: Role identity processes in retirement transition. *Journal of Organizational Behavior, 41*, 445–460. https://doi.org/10.1002/job.2438

Christiaens, A. H., Nelemans, S. A., Meeus, W. H., & Branje, S. (2021). Identity development across the transition from secondary to tertiary education: A 9-wave longitudinal study. *Journal of Adolescence, 93*, 245–256. https://doi.org/10.1016/j.adolescence.2021.03.007

den Boer, L., De Moor, E. L., & Reitz, A. K. (2026). Shaping who we are: Linking narratives to identity processes during the university-to-work transition. *European Journal of Personality, 40*, 111–125. https://doi.org/10.1177/08902070241309490

de Moor, E. L., & Branje, S. (2023). Examining secondary school choice processes as a predictor of adjustment after the school transition. *Journal of Research on Adolescence*, *33*, 251–268. https://doi.org/10.1111/jora.12801

de Moor, E. L., van der Graaff, J., & Branje, S. (2023). Identity development across the transition from primary to secondary school: The role of personality and the social context. *Self and Identity, 22*, 762–782. https://doi.org/10.1080/15298868.2023.2196087

Erikson, E. H. (1950/1993). *Childhood and society*. Norton.

Giannone, Z. A., Haney, C. J., Kealy, D., & Ogrodniczuk, J. S. (2017). Athletic identity and psychiatric symptoms following retirement from varsity sports. *International Journal of Social Psychiatry*, 63, 598–601. https://doi.org/10.1177/0020764017724184

Haslam, C., Lam, B. C. P., Branscombe, N. R., Steffens, N. K., Haslam, S. A., Cruwys, T., Fong, P., & Ball, T. C. (2018). Adjusting to life in retirement: The protective role of new group memberships and identification as a retiree. *European Journal of Work and Organizational Psychology, 27*, 822–839. https://doi.org/10.1080/1359432X.2018.1538127

Haslam, C., Lam, B. C. P., Yang, J., Steffens, N. K., Haslam, S. A., Cruwys, T., Boen, F., Mertens, N., De Brandt, K., Wang, X., Mallett, C. J., & Fransen, K. (2021). When the final whistle blows: Social identity pathways support mental health and life satisfaction after retirement from competitive sport. *Psychology of Sport and Exercise, 57*, 1–12. https://doi.org/10.1016/j.psychsport.2021.102049

Kunnen, E. S. (2023). The role of emotional experiences in commitment development in internship students. *Identity, 23*, 379–393. https://doi.org/10.1080/15283488.2023.2235392

Luyckx, K., Duriez, B., Klimstra, T. A., & De Witte, H. (2010). Identity statuses in young adult employees: Prospective relations with work engagement and burnout. *Journal of Vocational Behavior, 77*, 339–349. https://doi.org/10.1016/j.jvb.2010.06.002

Mannerström, R., Muotka, J., & Salmela-Aro, K. (2019). Associations between identity processes and success in developmental tasks during the transition from emerging to young adulthood. *Journal of Youth Studies, 22*, 1289–1307. https://doi.org/10.1080/13676261.2019.1571179

Scott, K. S. (2022). Making sense of work: finding meaning in work narratives. *Journal of Management & Organization, 28*, 1057–1077. https://doi.org/10.1017/jmo.2019.43

Skorikov, V. B., & Vondracek, F. W. (2011). Occupational Identity. In: Schwartz, S., Luyckx, K., & Vignoles, V. (Eds.). *Handbook of Identity Theory and Research*. Springer. https://doi.org/10.1007/978-1-4419-7988-9_29

Turner, K., Lilgendahl, J. P., Syed, M., & McLean, K. C. (2024). Testing exploratory narrative processing as a mechanism of change in identity status processes over 4 years in college-going emerging adults. *Developmental Psychology, 60*, 59–74. https://doi.org/10.1037/dev0001665

Weller, J. A., de Moor, E. L., & Klimstra, T. A. (2026). Age patterns in dual-cycle identity processes and their associations with life satisfaction. *Journal of Personality, 94*, 304–319. https://doi.org/10.1111/jopy.70001

Chapter 12

Identity development and policy

Many years ago, I was one of the professors in a two-week international intensive program on identity development sponsored by the European Union. There were students from six different countries: Italy, Lithuania, Portugal, Sweden, The Netherlands, and Türkiye. In addition to having the chance to learn about identity development, they also learned about other countries and cultures, and by being among students from other countries also about their own cultural identity. Despite differences between countries, there are many common values, and these programs illuminate those as well. In other words, they also facilitate building a European identity, and research on related exchange programs suggests they can be effective in reaching this goal (Bobba et al., 2024). Such efforts sponsored by the European Union aren't just causing such effects on identity by accident, as strengthening a sense of European identity is literally included in the program's general aims (European Commission, 2025). So, governmental organizations sometimes seek to promote identity development, in this case the development of a European identity, through policy.

There are a range of other **policies** in place that can boost development of a particular part of our identity. For example, government policies that give people a day off on their national holiday can boost a feeling of national identity. Other organizations do it, too. Think of the mascots that many U.S. universities and colleges have and put on their merchandise. Those have been chosen consciously as it matters for how much of a boost it gives to students' and

Policies Sets of procedures, guidelines or rules set by organizations such as governments, schools, and businesses, or individuals. These influence what individuals are able, unable, encouraged, and discouraged to do.

DOI: 10.4324/9781003557593-16

professors' college identity. For example, appointing a mighty elephant as a mascot instead of, for example, a rat[1], probably makes a difference for how much you'd want to identify with a college or university.

The previous examples were all rather simple and direct takes on how policy can boost a specific identity aspect. The broader aspects of identity development that this book mainly focuses on are also affected by policies. This chapter focuses on the link of identity development more broadly with policies for education, work, and navigating multiple roles such as work- and family-related ones.

Shaping educational systems

The previous chapter (Chapter 11) discusses school transitions in The Netherlands involving the necessity to make decisions with career implications by the end of elementary school. Several other countries (e.g., Germany, Türkiye, China) also require youth to make such decisions during adolescence, for example regarding the type of education (e.g., vocational, academic) or what school subjects they want to focus on. Not all of them have to make such decisions by age 12 though. While school-related career decisions aren't always as definitive as they might seem, they can sure feel that way for both youth and their caregivers. So, given what we know about identity development, how reasonable is it to expect an 11-, 12-, or even 15-year-old to make such decisions? A first way to answer this question would be to simply think back to what you were like at those ages. Did you know what you wanted to do career-wise? And even if that was the case, does what you wanted to do back then correspond to what you are doing now?

There is also research suggesting what could be a reasonable age to ask youth to make career decisions. That is not going to be the same age everywhere. It can make sense to promote early decisions if the transition into the job market is early, so by age 16 or so, or if there is less of a cultural emphasis on choosing a specific career and more of a tradition to take over one's parents' job. However, commitments aren't necessarily stable in adolescence (Klimstra et al., 2010) and youth in their late teens and early 20s are still very likely to explore, often even more so than younger adolescents (Luyckx et al., 2013). In other words, people in their 20s are often still figuring out what they want to do with their life. Added to that, identity development has been associated with the development of the pre-frontal cortex (Becht et al., 2018), which, at least in rich Western countries that offer prolonged education, is known to extend well through adolescence and into young adulthood (Blakemore & Mills, 2014). This all would make it seem logical to have policies that don't require 11- or 12-year-olds to make important educational decisions. Interestingly, unlike in countries like The Netherlands and Germany, countries like the United States and the United Kingdom do promote such later decisions. As the educational systems in the United Kingdom and United States have different problems, it is hard to say who is doing things right, but research on identity development does strongly point to the desirability of postponing career decisions to at least the late teens.

Policies promoting career flexibility, multiple roles, and multiple identities

I still remember the contract I got back in 2015, which said that I'd be employed until 2049. Much like many people who long for a permanent contract, I initially thought that was great as I would never have to worry about getting another job anymore. But, a little later I couldn't help starting to have some feelings that were more like "so this is it for the rest of my career, for another 34 years". In other words, despite its obvious benefits, long-term contracts can make you feel a bit trapped in your position, at least it did for me. Depending on your personal situation and factors such as your identity style (normative, diffuse-avoidant, or information-oriented; see Chapter 5), such feelings may or may not come up for you. There are various ways in which they can be navigated, with governmental and/or employers' policies being related to the options that are available.

Broader socioeconomic policy

For those who develop feelings of being stuck with their job, societal factors influenced by government policy can make a difference. For example, part of why the research covered in the previous chapter (Mannerström et al., 2019) showed that leaving a job decreased rather than increased such worries may have been because the study was conducted in Finland. Finland has a strong economy and a socioeconomic system in which inhabitants are taxed relatively heavily (OECD, 2025) but get good social security in return. In other words, there is a safety net that reduces the financial uncertainty associated with leaving your job and moving into a riskier entrepreneurial or other endeavor. In countries with fewer resources and/or a less strong social security system, such a safety net may not be available, which would make leaving a job a rather risky thing to do. As a result, people may be more inclined to keep jobs that they aren't satisfied with. It is hard to stay committed to something you're not satisfied with, and a decline in commitment along with feeling like you can't explore much resembles moving towards a diffusion status which has been linked to burnout symptoms (Luyckx et al., 2010). Therefore, countries that have the resources to provide a social safety net could consider investing more in this to avoid making people gravitate towards identity diffusion and, with that, burnout. In other words, even broader socioeconomic policy can impact identity development and its effects on workers' well-being.

Policies promoting part-time work

Many people don't necessarily want to leave their job but feel like they are doing too much of the same thing for too much of their time. For these people, governments and employers can work together to stimulate their identity development, and with that their well-being and job engagement. An important target could be the (im)possibility of having a part-time job. In some countries, like the United States, it can be hard or at least unattractive to work any less than full-time. Job-related benefits such as having healthcare coverage may only be available for full-timers, part-time work might be less rewarded with per-hour salaries being lower, or reducing working hours is not possible at all due to employer policies. As a result, part-time jobs are rare for some professions. In contrast, in other countries, such as those in Northern Europe, policies are different with, for example, healthcare benefits being less dependent on having a full-time job. As a result, many people are able to reduce their hours for a particular job at various points in their life. They have a variety of motives for this.

One motive is to find another job next to one's current job, or to become partly self-employed. You might struggle to come up with an example of someone who holds multiple jobs, but at universities it's not uncommon. In fact, various of the professors I know in the field of identity research hold professional appointments next to their professorships. A common example is an appointment as a clinician, but others were trained as a chef in a restaurant or successfully pursued a career as a singer-songwriter. They are not alone in this as a subgroup of people really thrive when they have multiple jobs (Bouwhuis et al., 2019). Of course, there are also plenty of people who aren't happy when they have multiple jobs, so nobody should be forced to do so. It really is offering the possibility to pursue multiple jobs that can be desirable from a societal perspective.

Having multiple jobs doesn't have to negatively affect people's income as the hours of two part-time jobs can still add up to be equal to one full-time job. An advantage is that if people who hold multiple jobs lose one, they might be able to increase their hours in the other job. In other words, people with two part-time jobs may be more resilient against downturns in a particular sector of the economy. Take, for example, those who worked in the cassette tape industry, but were also trained for, or perhaps even had another part-time job in, another industry. They likely were better off when cassette tapes were replaced by CDs. If you don't know what cassettes and CDs are[2], that would prove the point I am trying to make: times do change and as a result of that, jobs can disappear. Being trained for multiple jobs can have some benefits under those circumstances. At a governmental level, training people for multiple jobs can be stimulated by offering part-time education at a reduced price or even for free. Some governments, such as the U.S. state of Massachusetts, have such policies and offers free community college training to people over 25 years old (Mass.gov, n.d.). Of course, combining education with a job is hard when those are full-time. However, the policy itself does align with research findings that people continue to do identity exploration into their mid-to-late 20s (Luyckx et al., 2013) and that they therefore might want to get additional education.

Policies promoting part-time work also make it easier for people to combine their job role with a family role, particularly parenting. In research conducted in Sweden, where it is more common to work part-time, participants directly mentioned reducing work time as a way to become a more involved parent (Svensson & Frisén, 2022). That research specifically focused on people in their 30s who indicated that both work and family were central to how they saw themselves, so to their identity: they had what is called a **dual-centric identity**. Compared to people to whom neither work nor family or just one of the two were important they weren't necessarily happier in general, but they were happier with their job. Of course there were also downsides to a dual-centric identity, such as feelings of guilt about not being able to spend what felt like enough time on either their job or family, and burnout-related issues. Nonetheless, policies that allow for the possibility to work part-time have considerable benefits to enhance people's experience in combining work and family life.

> **Dual-centric identity** If someone does not consider one aspect of their identity more important than another, but considers two aspects (e.g., their work and parent identity) equally important, then they have a dual-centric identity.

Identity negotiation and policy

While this book mostly focuses on more general identity processes, it is crucial to also recognize that organizational and governmental policies affect how comfortable people feel expressing specific parts of their identity. In addition to what was already covered in this chapter, such aspects include sexual identity, gender identity, religious identity, political identity, social class identity, and ethnic-racial identity. Policies in organizations such as schools, but also at the (national) government level, can affect how comfortable people feel expressing a range of aspects of their identities. If people feel uncomfortable doing so and feel like they need to hide parts of their identity or drastically adapt the way they present themselves in different settings or to different people, this can negatively affect mental health (Galliher et al., 2025). That is why policies promoting inclusive practices are very important. Given the different values that are associated with different identities, even figuring out what leads to the optimal level of inclusiveness in a particular setting can be complicated. However, it is a key issue to address as an inclusive environment gives everyone equal chances to thrive.

Conclusion

Overall, there is much potential for utilizing research on identity development to inform policy. This chapter only scratched the surface. It is important to keep in mind that not every policy will benefit everyone equally, so for much of what has been discussed in this chapter it is a matter of creating different opportunities for different people to follow their desired path. Beyond that, what works and what doesn't depends on the context such as the country, school, company, classroom, and so on. In other words, policies can affect identity development in beneficial ways, but before implementing any policy it is necessary to carefully consider the potential consequences for everyone involved.

Notes

1 Nothing against rats, but they just aren't usually very popular with people. They're very smart, though, but perhaps their innovative ways of getting into garbage and other food sources have done more harm than good to their reputation.

2 To satisfy your potential curiosity: CDs and cassettes are (in present tense, as some of us still have them . . .) devices people use to store their music or other audio on.

Further sources

1. The Pursuit of Happyness; https://www.imdb.com/title/tt0454921/

   Movie about a man who struggles with balancing his professional career with raising his child. It is a good illustration of how difficult it can be to balance different aspects of our identity, if there are few policies that help people navigate such double roles. And no, I did not misspell "happiness", it's actually called happyness in the title of the movie.

2. Brown, T., Scrase, T. J., & Ganguly-Scrase, R. (2017) Globalised dreams, local constraints: migration and youth aspirations in an Indian regional town. *Children's Geographies, 15*, 531–544. https://doi.org/10.1080/14733285.2016.1274948

   Article written in an accessible way, describing how globalization (which is driven by local and international policy) brings about complexities in the career development of youth living in a town in Northern India. There are always some tensions between local culture and broader culture, so wherever you're from, you can probably at least somewhat relate to the complexities faced by the youth described in the article.

References

Becht, A. I., Bos, M. G., Nelemans, S. A., Peters, S., Vollebergh, W. A., Branje, S. J. T., Meeus, W. H. J., & Crone, E. A. (2018). Goal-directed correlates and neurobiological underpinnings of adolescent identity: A multimethod multisample longitudinal approach. *Child Development, 89*, 823–836. https://doi.org/10.1111/cdev.13048

Blakemore, S. J., & Mills, K. L. (2014). Is adolescence a sensitive period for sociocultural processing? *Annual Review of Psychology, 65*, 187–207. https://doi.org/10.1146/annurev-psych-010213-115202

Bobba, B., De Lise, F., Klimstra, T. A., & Crocetti, E. (2024). Exploring the self, others, and the world: the interplay between experiences abroad in adolescence, identity processes, and ethnic prejudice. *Applied Developmental Science*, 1–21. https://doi.org/10.1080/10888691.2024.2407884

Bouwhuis, S., Hoekstra, T., Bongers, P. M., Boot, C. R. L., Geuskens, G. A., & van der Beek, A. J. (2019). Distinguishing groups and exploring health differences among multiple job holders aged 45 years and older. *International Archives of Occupational and Environmental Health, 92*, 67–79. https://doi.org/10.1007/s00420-018-1351-2

European Commission (2025, July 21). *Introduction – Erasmus+ Programme Guide.* Erasmus+. https://erasmus-plus.ec.europa.eu/programme-guide/erasmus-programme-guide/introduction

Galliher, R. V., Parmenter, J. G., Pradell, L. R., & Klimstra, T. (2025). Development and validation of the identity negotiation experiences and strategies scale. *Identity, 25*, 373–391. https://doi.org/10.1080/15283488.2024.2377171

Klimstra, T. A., Hale III, W. W., Raaijmakers, Q. A. W., Branje, S. J. T., & Meeus, W. H. J. (2010). Identity formation in adolescence: Change or stability? *Journal of Youth and Adolescence, 39*, 150–162. https://doi.org/10.1007/s10964-009-9401-4

Luyckx, K., Duriez, B., Klimstra, T. A., & De Witte, H. (2010). Identity statuses in young adult employees: Prospective relations with work engagement and burnout. *Journal of Vocational Behavior, 77*, 339–349. https://doi.org/10.1016/j.jvb.2010.06.002

Luyckx, K., Klimstra, T. A., Duriez, B., Van Petegem, S., & Beyers, W. (2013). Personal identity processes from adolescence through the late 20s: Age trends, functionality, and depressive symptoms. *Social Development, 22*, 701–721. https://doi.org/10.1111/sode.12027

Mannerström, R., Muotka, J., & Salmela-Aro, K. (2019). Associations between identity processes and success in developmental tasks during the transition from emerging to young adulthood. *Journal of Youth Studies, 22*, 1289–1307. https://doi.org/10.1080/13676261.2019.1571179

Mass.gov. (n.d.). Free community college. Commonwealth of Massachusetts. https://www.mass.gov/info-details/free-community-college

OECD (2025). *Taxing Wages 2025: Decomposition of Personal Income Taxes and the Role of Tax Reliefs*, OECD Publishing. https://doi.org/10.1787/b3a95829-en

Svensson, Y., & Frisén, A. (2022). Dual-centric work/family identity in young adults. *Self and Identity, 21*, 848–875. https://doi.org/10.1080/15298868.2021.1950828

Section 5

Key emerging areas

By the end of this section, you will:

- Know about person-specific research and how it can help us understand how the unique circumstances of specific people influence the effects of identity and their functioning.
- Appreciate that what is "good" about identity for some, or under some circumstances, is not necessarily "good" for others, or under different circumstances.
- Understand how the use of different types of digital technology can affect identity development, and how identity development may affect the use of different types of digital technology.

DOI: 10.4324/9781003557593-17

Chapter 13

Considering people's unique circumstances and experiences

Now that you have arrived in the final section of the book, you should have an idea about what is known about identity development, and what ideas have been getting a lot of attention. However, several things that are known to be important have only recently become more of a focus area: so-called emerging areas. This section of the book covers two such areas. In this chapter, the focus is on the growing area of research addressing the importance of considering the context in which people develop their identity. The next chapter will focus on the links between identity development and the use of various forms of digital technology including social media.

It has long been recognized that people don't just develop in a vacuum. Instead, we're affected by people and things around us. Classic work described in Chapter 4, such as theorizing by Erikson and Freud, indicates that what is available in society in terms of social roles and norms affects identity development. Yet, there hasn't been all that much reflection on whether things truly work the same for everyone, or whether the context or situation they're in matters. For example, can we truly say that one identity status or style is always "better" than others? Identity researchers are slowly gaining a better understanding of these issues as you've already been able to read in previous chapters. Chapter 5, for instance, covered several ideas of how each of the identity styles and each of the identity statuses can be adaptive depending on the environment and situation you're in. Chapter 10 also applied such ideas to commitment and exploration, covering that what you're committed to and how you're exploring matter for whether those are adaptive things to do. The rest of this chapter consists of three sections. First, current efforts to use **person-specific research**

> **Person-specific research** Research with a focus on specific individuals instead of on general patterns in larger groups of people.

DOI: 10.4324/9781003557593-18

to add nuance to generalizations on how identity development works are covered. The second section addresses how and why it is increasingly acknowledged that certain aspects of identity, such as specific identity styles or statuses, can't be simply described as "good" or "bad". The focus in the third and final section is on master narratives, as these widely held and shared beliefs, in the form of scripts within cultures, are increasingly studied to examine their effects on identity development.

Adding person-specific research to the mix

Identity development is about how we become unique and distinct individuals, so you would think that there would be widespread recognition that identity aspects have unique effects for specific individuals. However, that hasn't always necessarily been the case. This is changing, as there has been an increase in person-specific research.

To understand why person-specific research is important, we'll need to cover a bit of research methods and statistics. Don't worry though, there'll be no equations or letters from the Greek alphabet. The key thing to understand is that most research focuses on how between-person differences in one thing are related to between-person differences in another thing. For example, the positive identity commitment-anxiety link that is typically found in research means that the people who have lower levels of commitment tend to be the ones who are more likely to be among the people with higher levels of anxiety. Importantly, those associations don't mean that we can just recommend all people to become more committed to increase their well-being, because we don't know whether increased commitment leads to higher well-being for specific individuals. All we know is that people who are more committed are more likely to have higher levels of well-being than those who aren't as committed. In the last decade or so, researchers have been paying more attention to the nuances in general patterns by conducting so called within-person, or person-specific, studies. Perhaps this is best explained first with research that is not on identity, but on weather and mood.

To study the link between weather and mood, researchers also long relied on between-person associations. This means that they had some people filling out mood surveys when the weather was good (nice temperature, sunny) and others when the weather was bad (rainy, cold). Such research typically showed that those who were surveyed on days with bad weather reported having an equally good (or bad) mood compared to those who were surveyed on days with better weather. This was then sometimes interpreted as weather not having a measurable effect on mood, which is a problem for various reasons. To keep it close to real life: you probably know some people who are very much affected by the weather and some who aren't. In fact, you might even know some people who are happy when the sun is out and others who seem to be happier when it rains, so two groups of people with opposing reactions to the weather! Between-person studies cannot get to such nuances, as they're suitable for drawing one general conclusion on the relationship between two variables (e.g., weather and mood). They can't be used to examine whether change in the mood of a particular person is related to changes in the weather. For that, you need person-specific research. What you do then is gather data on weather and mood in the same group of people across several days. In one such study (Klimstra et al., 2011), we followed a group of adolescents and their moms for 30 days. We asked them about their mood, and we got the weather data for all 30 days. Next, we examined how weather was related to mood for each individual in our study. We found that for many people, their mood wasn't really related to the weather, that there were some who got a better mood with better weather, but also some who got a better mood when it was colder.

Identity researchers have started using such person-specific research as well, for example to see whether there's individual differences in how commitment change is related to emotions (van der Gaag et al., 2017). What they found is that the occurrence of both positive and negative emotions can be related to increases in commitment, but not for everyone. Why is not yet clear, but again the context, or, to make it more concrete, the personal situation of individuals may explain whether and to what extent their emotional experiences matter for change in their commitments. Currently, clarifying the "when", "how", and "for whom" of relationships between aspects of identity and everything it's known to be related to is a topic drawing a good bit of interest and it'll likely continue to be so in the decades to come. That's not to say that we now all deny that there's general patterns of findings that apply to many, because those are still of interest, too! The more individualized approach is a necessary addition as it allows for more nuance and therefore more accuracy, by acknowledging that identity development may work somewhat differently for different people.

Keep in mind that person-specific studies are very important, but that doesn't mean that research focusing on more general patterns shouldn't be done anymore. The focus is just different, in some specific technical ways not covered here as well. The key thing to remember is that the two types of approaches complement each other: we need to know about general patterns and about specific individuals, especially if they don't follow those general patterns.

"Good" and "bad"

Things may not just work differently for different people within your classroom, family, or friend group. There are also broader **generalizability** issues. As mentioned in Chapter 2, much of the research in psychology has been conducted on a very limited set of people: primarily college students from the United States, other English-speaking countries, and (Western) European countries. Research on identity development is no exception to that, so even established links between identity and "good" things like well-being may only apply to a select part of the world population.

> **Generalizability** The extent to which results from one study can be used to draw conclusions about a broader population. It also deals with issues about to which broader population results apply.

Related to this, there are also issues with considering things universally "good" or "bad". For example, committing to something that might seem to get you ahead in life could be paired with high levels of well-being (in the form of happiness) for you. However, it could harm others around you if it is directly at the expense of them. So, what is good for you isn't always good for the larger group. If you alienate the people you know with choices that are selfish, the initial increase in happiness caused by your new commitment may in the longer run turn into a decrease in happiness due to losing support from the people you know. Added to that, there's the even more complicated issue that seeing happiness as the key indicator of well-being has been described as a largely Western European and North American idea. Other ways of thinking, that cover ideas from a wider range of cultures, point out that well-being can also be indicated by, for example, meaning, spirituality, and harmony (Krys et al., 2025). Related to this, identity development itself doesn't work the same in every context (see Chapter 2 for examples on how things may work in some specific cultures outside of North America and Western Europe). Key to remember here is that the idea that exploration and following your own self-chosen path in life are the most important ways to figuring out who you are, doesn't necessarily fit with every culture around the world.

Differences between people aren't just related to culture. People are also different in terms of the political and economic (in)stability they experience, how much money they have available, how safe their neighborhood is, and many other contextual factors. In the last few years, this has already led some researchers to refrain from saying that one identity style or status is the best for everyone and to explain why something that generally works out "badly" can still be "good" for some. In Chapter 5, research was discussed that pointed to why a diffuse-avoidant identity style, which typically is associated with poor well-being, can actually be adaptive under some conditions. Those conditions include ones where the person doesn't have all that much to choose from or when making longer-term plans doesn't make a lot of sense. So again, context matters for whether something about identity should be considered "good" or "bad".

Then there is the issue that what is helpful at one age isn't always helpful at another age. Research from Belgium showed that exploration in breadth (comparing different identity options before committing, see Chapter 5) wasn't related to mental health among adolescents and people in their early 20s (Luyckx et al., 2013). However, it was associated with mental health problems among people in their late 20s. This may be because attempts to find something to commit to and trying different things is something that is appreciated by others when you're an adolescent or college student, but less so when you're nearing your thirties, when you're more expected to already have commitments in place. Another study, on narrative identity in early adolescent boys in the United States, focused on meaning making (McLean et al., 2010). Typically, narrative identity research shows that those with more sophisticated meaning making in their narratives have the highest levels of well-being. However, for early adolescent boys more sophisticated meaning making was associated with lower self-esteem and higher levels of depression. According to the authors, this may be because sophisticated attempts to find meaning in events is typically something we only do later in life, so when it's done early in adolescence it may be out of necessity. In other words, these boys may have gone through traumatic events that they needed to process. The traumatic events themselves may then explain the negative impact on well-being. With that, this study showed that meaning making isn't always a marker for positive well-being. Long story short: what applies to people of a certain age, doesn't necessarily apply to people of another age.

The main implication of everything covered in this section is that identity statuses, styles, dimensions, aspects of narrative identity, or just anything else identity-related cannot simply be described as "good" or "bad". There are many interesting ways in which the same thing that is "bad" for one person can work out in a "good" way for another person. Finding out how and why that is, is an emerging area in the study of identity development. Beyond what has already been discussed, one type of research really stands out as being a good example of examining the context, its effects on identity development, and its effects on what is considered "good" or "bad": research on master narratives.

Master narratives

As explained in Chapter 2, master narratives are culturally shared stories used by people to frame their own life stories. A clear example is the American Dream, which is about the belief that everyone has the chance to be successful in obtaining a good life through hard work. So, master narratives aren't necessarily stories of the traditional kind and also aren't necessarily "truths". Instead, they are widely held beliefs that are sometimes so deeply embedded in the culture that people aren't even fully aware of their existence. Next to master narratives, there are alternative narratives, that question the accuracy of master narratives. For example, for the American Dream, alternative narratives would argue that structural barriers make obtaining a good and wealthy life much harder for some compared to others, depending on factors such as gender, race, ethnicity, and social class. Both master and alternative narratives are thought to have large impacts on our narrative identity. These impacts have become a major topic of interest.

As an example of research on master narratives, one study focused on how 18 to 29-year-old white people in the United States described a good life (Schwab, 2020). Historically, things like marriage, a full-time job, and having children may have come up, but not as much in this study. Participants consistently emphasized that they thought that different people would have different ideas about what a good life was, so that their own ideas about a good life wouldn't necessarily correspond with those of others. That indicates that they believed that every person has unique needs and desires, which already is a master narrative itself. The two other major themes that consistently came up were independence and interdependence, which together point to "the good life" being one in which you decide things for yourself, are self-sufficient, but still maintain good connections with others and the world around you. Given the consistency in the responses of the participants, there appeared to be a master narrative on what "the good life" was according to American young adults: one that was unique to each individual but with a mix of independence and interdependence.

We might all want "the good life", but sometimes people encounter adverse or even traumatic experiences. When they tell stories to make sense of those experiences, they also rely on master narratives. Which ones those are was examined among young adults in the United Kingdom (Blackie et al., 2023). People in the United States are known to frequently rely on the redemption master narrative. That means that even negative stories end on a positive note, as they add how they overcame the challenge or learned something from the negative experience. That may sound like most of the Hollywood movies you've watched, which further underscores the point that using redemption to frame a story is a widespread practice in the United States, so, a master narrative. While some stories regarding adversity were still narrated in a redemptive way in the United Kingdom, stories that aligned more with a recuperation theme were the most common: they were used by almost everyone! Recuperation even had a particular sequence to it, starting with an adverse reaction, followed by active coping strategies (so active and productive ways of emotionally dealing with what happened), which then were followed by actual recuperation in the form of getting past the adverse reaction. So, the consistently used cultural script, or master narrative, in the United Kingdom that prescribes how one is expected to talk about processing adverse events is one of recuperation and not redemption, like it is in the United States. This illustrates the cultural nature of master narratives!

There are master narratives, and next to those also alternative narratives, on a whole lot of other topics, such as what a family is supposed to be like or about how you're supposed to pick a career, but also ones regarding sexuality, gender, race and ethnicity, religiosity, and pretty much everything else you can think of. These master and alternative narratives, and their effects on the narratives of individuals who follow or deviate from them, are increasingly being studied. Given the number of topics that master narratives apply to, the cultural specificity of them, the fact that they can differ by generation, and that they only recently have gotten more attention, this will likely remain a frequently studied and debated topic in the years to come.

Conclusion

This chapter covered the emerging area of knowledge on how the context that people live in needs to be considered when we try to make sense of their identity development. Remember that while it is important to consider people's unique situation, circumstances, position in society, and cultural context, there are also still things that do apply to larger groups of people. For example, having strong identity commitments is still associated with higher levels of happiness among most young people in English-speaking and (Western) European countries. The most important thing to remember about this new emerging area of knowledge is that what applies to many doesn't necessarily apply to everyone, and that what generally seems to be "good" for people isn't always "good" for everyone in every way or under all circumstances.

Lastly, keep in mind that we are influenced by master narratives and the norms and values they come with. Even if you resist master narratives by adopting alternatives, you are in a way still affected by them because you'd be reacting to them. Clearly, things are complicated and not always what they look like. This is what makes research on identity development so fascinating for people whose job it is to understand it in all its complexities. I hope that you'll be fascinated by it as well!

Further sources

1. Lorena, Light-footed Woman; https://www.imdb.com/title/tt11162992/

   Short documentary about a young woman who lives in a remote, rural part of Mexico, and is a successful ultramarathon runner. However, she does this in what would seem like an unconventional way to people from areas that are more affected by globalization. This illustrates how her unique circumstances affect her identity. At times, she clearly struggles with the two different worlds, and different master narratives, she needs to navigate.

2. McLean, K. C. (2024). *Why change is hard: The power of master narratives over self and society.* Oxford University Press.

   A book that provides an accessible and in-depth analysis of how master narratives and the societal norms they communicate affect our identities and make it hard to make changes. It primarily draws from the narrative identity perspective that is extensively discussed in Chapters 4 and 8 of this book (the one you're currently reading).

References

Blackie, L. E. R., Colgan, J. E. V., McDonald, S., & McLean, K. C. (2023). A qualitative investigation into the cultural master narrative for overcoming trauma and adversity in the United Kingdom. *Qualitative Psychology, 10*, 154–170. https://doi.org/10.1037/qup0000163

Klimstra, T. A., Frijns, T., Keijsers, L., Denissen, J. J. A., Raaijmakers, Q. A. W., van Aken, M. A. G., Koot, H. M., van Lier, P. A. C., & Meeus, W. H. J. (2011). Come rain or come shine: Individual differences in how weather affects mood. *Emotion, 11*, 1495–1499. https://doi.org/10.1037/a0024649

Krys, K., Kostoula, O., van Tilburg, W. A. P., Mosca, O., Lee, J. H., Maricchiolo, F., Kosiarczyk, A., Kocimska-Bortnowska, A., Torres, C., Hitokoto, H., Liew, K., Bond, M. H., Lun, V. M.-C., Vignoles, V. L., Zelenski, J. M., Haas, B. W., Park, J., Vauclair, C.-M., Kwiatkowska,

A., . . . & Uchida, Y. (2025). Happiness maximization is a WEIRD way of living. *Perspectives on Psychological Science, 20*, 874–902. https://doi.org/10.1177/17456916231208367

Luyckx, K., Klimstra, T. A., Duriez, B., Van Petegem, S., & Beyers, W. (2013). Personal identity processes from adolescence through the late 20s: Age trends, functionality, and depressive symptoms. *Social Development, 22*, 701–721. https://doi.org/10.1111/sode.12027

McLean, K. C., Breen, A. V., & Fournier, M. A. (2010). Constructing the self in early, middle, and late adolescent boys: Narrative identity, individuation, and well-being. *Journal of Research on Adolescence, 20*, 166–187. https://doi.org/10.1111/j.1532-7795.2009.00633.x

Schwab, J. R. (2020). What is the good life? A master narrative approach to the study of morals and values in American emerging adults. *Journal of Adult Development, 27*, 108–117. https://doi.org/10.1007/s10804-019-09329-w

Thalmayer, A. G., Toscanelli, C., & Arnett, J. J. (2021). The neglected 95% revisited: Is American psychology becoming less American? *American Psychologist, 76*, 116–129. https://doi.org/10.1037/amp0000622

van der Gaag, M., Albers, C., & Kunnen, S. (2017). Micro-level mechanisms of identity development: The role of emotional experiences in commitment development. *Developmental Psychology, 53*, 2205–2217. https://doi.org/10.1037/dev0000336

Chapter 14

Digital technology and identity development

During my childhood in the 1980s and 1990s, there were no mobile phones, no tablets, and the internet was unknown and unavailable to most people. When I was a teenager at some point, there was this kid coming to school with a mobile phone thinking he was cool. Me and my friends didn't think that he was, because who would he call while at school? His parents? Or would his parents just be able to call him anytime to check on him? That was the exact opposite of the freedom that we were starting to enjoy from our parents, so that wasn't cool at all! Needless to say, at that point I didn't think that many people would ever want to have a mobile phone[1]. This is just one example of my general proven uselessness in predicting the future, which led me to not write the chapters in this section about "future directions". Rather, I decided that a focus on rapidly expanding areas of research is a safer bet. One of those areas has to do with mobile phones: it's the role of digital technology in identity development. This chapter will focus on that role by taking a broad focus on various forms of digital technology including social media.

Smartphone use, video games, and social media have all been covered extensively in news media as major factors that "ruin today's youth". While there certainly are negative effects of digital tools, they also have benefits including ones directly relevant to identity development. Also, the fact that Erikson (1950/1993) was already writing about morality-related dangers of the life stage in which identity development is the central developmental task, shows that concerns about the next generation of youth aren't restricted to the present. As such, the goal for this chapter is to provide a balanced perspective pointing to both pros and cons of digital technology in its role in identity development. The first section will focus on how people explore their identity while engaging with digital technology, for example by trying out new roles and figuring out the different sides of themselves. The second section discusses how people develop their narrative identity in digital contexts. The third section covers how people seek to consolidate and clarify their identity

DOI: 10.4324/9781003557593-19

through self-presentation and finding people like them. The fourth and final section covers the Artificial Intelligence (AI) boom of the mid 2020s and how it may relate to identity development.

After reading this chapter, you should be familiar with research that has been done on the role of digital media in identity development and have an appreciation of this role being complex and not limited to specific forms of digital technology. This chapter seeks to refer to general principles of the role of digital media and not the effects of specific platforms. Therefore, you should be able to apply ideas on how identity may develop in a variety of digital platforms, some of which may not have even been around by the time this chapter was written (in 2025).

Identity exploration

Identity exploration is all about gathering information, sometimes to compare different options of where to go with your life, and sometimes also for evaluating your current commitments (see also Chapters 1 and 5). It's easy to see that digital technology plays a role in identity exploration as it provides access to an almost endless amount of information. Just think of our everyday use of phones, tablets, and other devices to look up things. Some of the information we encounter accidentally happens to be relevant to how we see ourselves, but people can also intentionally use digital technology when they are exploring their identity.

Of course, digital technology isn't always beneficial. Take, for example, excessive use of Social Networking Sites (SNS) such as Facebook, Instagram, TikTok, YouTube, and X, in other words repeatedly using those for more time than you planned and having a hard time stopping. Research showed an association between such excessive SNS use and lower levels of in-depth exploration (Imperato et al., 2023). That's likely because it takes time away from deeper reflection on life choices. It was also associated with higher levels of identity reconsideration, which in this case likely reflected doubt and not an active search for alternative commitments. However, most uses are not necessarily problematic, which is a good thing since billions of people use SNS!

Positive uses of SNS for exploration are often related to self-presentation (Avci et al., 2025). Some are pretty basic, like editing profiles and posting. Other uses include experimenting with different looks, roles, or even pretending to be someone else. People who reported more of those uses also reported engaging in more identity exploration. One could even make the argument that experimenting with one's identity on SNS is a form of identity exploration!

However, there's still a lot that isn't known about identity exploration on SNS, partly because all SNS are different. For example, Instagram stories disappear 24 hours after they're posted, whereas for Snapchat the default is for posts to disappear after they've been viewed once. All SNS also support different content, for example in terms of the length of posts, whether they support text, video, and/or images, and whether and how people can react. All these features affect how SNS can, and cannot, be used for identity expression and thus exploration. As many people use multiple SNS, but different people use different mixes, it gets pretty complicated to do research. On top of that, there's a constant need for new studies as new SNS continue to be added, and the existing ones continue to evolve. So, we're just at the beginning stages of getting an understanding of how identity exploration works on SNS.

Avatar One's virtual or in-game persona or character.

Videogames provide another platform for identity exploration. In many games, players use an **avatar**, which could simply be described as one's virtual or in-game persona (Wood & Szymanski, 2020). Such avatars can be customized to varying degrees, depending on the game one plays. This customization can include character features, such as their charisma, that lead to advantages and disadvantages while playing the game. While playing the game itself, there are further options on how to play a role. To just give one example: if you take on the role of a mayor of a city or the dictator of a country in a videogame, you can either go with policies in line with your moral and political convictions or do something different. From personal experience, I can share that not going with your moral convictions can be hard, even in a virtual world! If that's the case, that could mean that certain convictions are important to you, thereby clarifying your identity. In other cases, such experiences with avatars and gameplay can even serve as a way of figuring out who you might be able to become, so it might extend your repertoire of possible selves (see Chapter 3). Obviously, playing with different roles as a way of identity exploration predates the videogame era. However, videogames allow for relatively easy and elaborate experimentation and can therefore facilitate identity exploration.

Narrative identity development

Digital technology can also be used for storytelling. This can happen on SNS, in the chat of videogames, in fora such as Reddit, and sometimes even in instant messaging. Several chapters (Chapters 4 and 8) explain how storytelling is central to narrative identity development. What wasn't covered is how narrative identity development can play out in digital media.

Communion A person's motivation for being connected with others through specific bonds or through the feeling of being part of a larger group.

How this may work has been covered by researchers (Granic et al., 2020) who focused on the themes of agency and coherence (see Chapter 8), but also on **communion**. Communion refers to a person's motivation for being connected with others through specific bonds or through the feeling of being part of a larger group (Granic et al., 2020). Each of those themes play out in various digital contexts, but more clearly in some than in others.

Coherence is very relevant to how people present themselves across different SNS. It can be hard to play very different roles on different sites and still present yourself as a coherent person, especially if you're followed by the same people across those different sites. This is not to say that emphasizing different parts of who you are on different sites would mean you'd look incoherent to others or yourself. People have emphasized different sides of themselves in different roles for centuries, so presenting different sides of you on different SNS would just be a modern version of that. Especially if you manage to present those different pieces of yourself as part of a larger, coherent, puzzle, this may strengthen your narrative identity.

Narrative identity construction in a digital context also happens through videogames (Granic et al., 2020). The chat function in online multiplayer games offers one avenue for this and this is especially helpful in collaborative games. Chats can become very elaborate and take the form of stories. Some games directly emphasize social and emotional aspects and can do this so well that players feel compelled to share identity narratives regarding their experiences in online fora. Such stories often refer to a communal theme.

Overcoming difficulties in an agentic way, so, through your own efforts, is also a general theme in many videogames. As such, those games can also help us feel more agentic (Granic et al., 2020). Even just the very fact that there's a learning curve with pretty much any videogame, with challenges that initially seem impossible becoming manageable after a bit of practice, contributes to this sense of agency. Also, videogames can provide a sense of agency to people who aren't able to be agentic in other settings for whatever reason. In that way, games can contribute to self-worth, so, a more positive identity.

Of course, digital technology also has negative sides. The endless amount of information provided on websites, social media, and other platforms can be rather overwhelming and hard to make sense of (Granic et al., 2020). Also, the ease of finding information on almost anything within a couple of seconds can reduce the need and desire to figure out things in other ways, such as through trial and error. In other words, there is the risk of technology getting in the way of spontaneous creative problem solving, and that's in part what identity exploration is about. On top of that, the information we're provided with isn't neutral, can be incorrect, and can be different for different people. We'll return to that point later, but for now the key thing to remember is that the introduction and increased sophistication of digital technology is neither all negative, nor all positive, for identity development.

Identity consolidation and clarification

In Chapter 1, you learned that development isn't always about change. It can also be characterized by stability. Digital technology can contribute to such stability by helping us maintain our current identity or clarify particular identity aspects. There are several ways in which this can work.

One important way in which digital technology helps with clarifying and maintaining parts of our identity, is by allowing for access to a large audience that is not restricted to your immediate physical environment. Because of this, people with less common identity aspects in a particular area, such as those who are part of a minority based on ethnicity, sexuality, gender, or even based on an interest, can find people like themselves much more easily. A study on cultural identity among Hmong[2] American young adults in California, in the United States, illustrated how this may work (McKenzie, 2025). Specifically, several participants posted pictures of themselves in traditional Hmong clothing and music videos in Hmong language. Those actions were coupled with expression of frustration over language loss. Therefore, they could be interpreted not only as ways to keep their own identity in place, but also to safeguard the continuity of larger structures that identities are anchored in, such as, in this case, the Hmong culture.

Basically, digital technology gives us access to a broader range of conversation partners. When you are part of some group or community on social media or other online space that is tied to a specific interest, value, orientation, or other characteristic, you're likely to meet people with lived experiences similar to yours, increasing the chances that some of those people will be responsive to you. This is important because having responsive conversation partners tends to work out favorably for narrative identity development (Pasupathi & Hoyt, 2009). Without digital technology, accessing such helpful communal spaces would be a lot harder for those with identity aspects that are rare or even stigmatized in their immediate physical environment.

Current and future developments

I am writing this chapter in 2025 while the use of AI is growing very rapidly. The use of AI has potential implications for identity development, but it's too early to say anything definitive about that because there's a lack of research for now. Again, it's not good to only be alarmist about AI as some uses can lead to greater equity. For example, polishing grammar using AI is helpful for those who write in a language that is very different from their first language. This could lead to people's ideas being judged more for their merit and less for their mastery of the language.

However, there obviously are also potential downsides. The list presented here is not exhaustive but is based on issues that can be linked to identity theories or that attract considerable media attention. One issue has to do with algorithms, which put things on our social media feed that we supposedly like or are interested in, and keep things off our feed that we don't like or may disagree with. Several identity theories emphasize how important it is to get realistic feedback, which is not just positive, to figure out who we really are and who we're not. Identity control theory and identity negotiation theory (see Chapter 6) are among the clearest examples of such theories. Also, our identities are shaped by a socio-cultural context and with that also become adaptive to such a context. If algorithms feed us only information from one part of the broader context while ignoring other information, we'd only be able to relate to specific parts of the social world and not to others. Strong identification with some and strong distancing from others, so, polarization, might then be the result.

Somewhat related to this, there are chatbots. Those are programmed to mimic our tone to make us feel good and also to confirm our beliefs, including delusional ones (Wei, 2025). Therefore, there are growing concerns that they can contribute to psychoses. Again, the uncritical feedback of such chatbots can lead to skewed ideas of who we really are. However, how this all works exactly does still need to be examined in scientific studies.

There are also AI images and videos, and whole apps and platforms for making those (Brumfiel, 2025). These can make it look like a person did something outrageous or extraordinary even if they never did it. In other words, we could get feedback on who we are for things we never did. That may lead to frustration because of being misrepresented, but potentially also to identity confusion as one might take misguided feedback seriously.

Unfortunately, this section ended up being a bit alarmist. It's therefore important to mention that right now we don't know exactly how identity development will be affected by AI; we can only rely on theoretical predictions. Also, there definitely are potential good and productive uses. Dull repetitive things can likely be left to AI, which may allow many people to engage in more creative endeavors. That might then give them more chances to find out what their unique strengths and weaknesses are, thereby contributing to identity development.

Conclusion

Most people now live their life in constant interaction with digital technology. Rather than seeing that as good or bad, the goal should be to make sense of that reality and see how it affects our identity development. In this chapter, you read about research that is currently being done to better understand how identity development may be affected by Social Networking Sites, but also by videogames. There are many potential positive effects in addition to the negative effects that are widely covered in media. The widespread adoption of Artificial Intelligence-based technology is a very recent phenomenon but will likely have a similar mix of positive and negative effects on identity development. It will be important to not use AI to make ourselves be less authentic, as being yourself is fundamental to having a well-developed identity.

Notes

1 You could only call and text with mobile phones at that time as it would take another couple of years for mobile internet to become widely available.
2 The Hmong are an ethnic group indigenous to southern China.

Further sources

1. Granic, I., Morita, H., & Scholten, H. (2020). Beyond screen time: Identity development in the digital age. *Psychological Inquiry, 31*(3), 195–223. https://doi.org/10.1080/1047840X.2020.1820214

   Academic article, but a very accessible overview on how identity development is affected by digital technology. The article takes a nuanced approach to the role of digital technology, highlighting positive aspects. This is a nice contrast with popular books on this topic that primarily focus on the negative sides (see Jonathan Haidt's work, which I am personally less enthusiastic about).

2. The Berkman Klein Center for Internet and Society at Harvard University; https://cyber.harvard.edu/about

   Website of a research center entirely devoted to the role of digital technology in society. If you want to know about recent developments, you can check out their project, programs, and publications.

References

Avci, H., Baams, L. & Kretschmer, T. (2025). A systematic review of social media use and adolescent identity development. *Adolescent Research Review, 10*, 219–236. https://doi.org/10.1007/s40894-024-00251-1

Brumfiel, G. (2025). *Kiss reality goodbye: AI-generated social media has arrived.* NPR. https://www.npr.org/2025/10/03/nx-s1-5560200/openai-sora-social-media

Erikson, E. H. (1950/1993). *Childhood and society.* Norton.

Granic, I., Morita, H., & Scholten, H. (2020). Beyond screen time: Identity development in the digital age. *Psychological Inquiry, 31*(3), 195–223. https://doi.org/10.1080/1047840X.2020.1820214

Imperato, C., Mancini, T. & Musetti, A. (2023). Exploring the role of problematic social network site use in the link between reflective functioning and identity processes in adolescents. *International Journal of Mental Health and Addiction, 21*, 3430–3445. https://doi.org/10.1007/s11469-022-00800-6

McKenzie, J. (2025). Digital media as sites for cultural identity development: The case of Hmong American emerging adults. *Journal of Adolescent Research, 40*, 296–330. https://doi.org/10.1177/07435584221116312

Pasupathi, M., & Hoyt, T. (2009). The development of narrative identity in late adolescence and emergent adulthood: The continued importance of listeners. *Developmental Psychology, 45*, 558–574. https://doi.org/10.1037/a0014431

Wei, M. (2025, July 21). The emerging problem of "AI psychosis". *Psychology Today.* https://www.psychologytoday.com/us/blog/urban-survival/202507/the-emerging-problem-of-ai-psychosis

Wood, S. M., & Szymanski, A. (2020). "The Me I Want You to See": The use of video game avatars to explore identity in gifted adolescents. *Gifted Child Today, 43*, 124–134. https://doi.org/10.1177/1076217519898217

Index

www.ingramcontent.com/pod-product-compliance
Lightning Source LLC
Chambersburg PA
CBHW070244230726
48635CB00031B/430
* 9 7 8 1 0 3 2 9 0 2 1 5 9 *